I Was a Cold War Monster

I Was a Cold War Monster:

Horror Films, Eroticism, and the Cold War Imagination

Cyndy Hendershot

Bowling Green State University Popular Press
Bowling Green, OH 43403

Copyright 2001 © Bowling Green State University Popular Press

Library of Congress Cataloging-in-Publication Data

Hendershot, Cynthia.
    I was a cold war monster : horror films, eroticism, and the cold war
imagination / Cyndy Hendershot.
        p.   cm.
    Includes bibliographical references and index.
    ISBN 0-87972-849-3 (cloth) -- ISBN 0-87972-850-7 (paper)
    1. Horror films--History and criticism. I. Title.

PN1995.9.H6 H46 2001
791.43'614--dc21

                                          2001035614

Cover design by Dumm Art

For Antony with love

CONTENTS

ACKNOWLEDGMENTS

Thanks to Arkansas State University for grant money that helped make this book possible. Thanks as always to Miss D. and to Antony Oldknow, to whom this book is dedicated. Thanks to Jerry Ball for the use of his archive of horror films.

A version of Chapter 2 was published in *The Journal of Popular Film and Television* 29.1. A version of Chapter 6 appeared in *Quarterly Review of Film and Video* 17.3. A version of Chapter 7 appeared in *Images: A Journal of Film and Popular Culture.*

INTRODUCTION

In William Castle's 1959 horror film *The Tingler*, the tingler, an insect-like creature that grows on the spines of men or women when they experience fear, gets loose in a movie theater. Castle's film technique Percepto involved turning off all the lights in the theater in the course of the movie's action and simultaneously activating electrical buzzers that had been placed under some people's seats so that they would think the tingler was after them.[1] With its explicit construction of a very tangible metaphor for fear itself, *The Tingler* captured the spirit of fifties horror. The terror experienced by the characters in the film and by the audience in the movie theater is fear in its primal form.

Fifties horror speaks to an amorphous fear much like that embodied in the tingler itself, one unleashed on its original audience in a darkened movie theater or in a car at a drive-in. Yet, horror fiction's monsters assumed forms that were very recognizable within the context of cold war America. Beneath the seemingly universal terror of werewolves and vampires, lurked very real and contemporary concerns about communists and juvenile delinquents.

In this study, I read fifties horror films, from both the United States and Britain, within the framework of social discourses that attempted to understand a society beset by fears of infiltration both from without and from within. Postwar Americans and Britons feared very real monsters that might well be lurking around the corner, and these horrors found cinematic expression in the monsters of horror film. Some were familiar monsters, like werewolves, mummies, and vampires; others were creatures of the new atomic age, mutations such as giant gila monsters and amazing colossal men.

Sociologists of the cold war era saw monsters everywhere. Whether they were Lewis Mumford's government and military zombies leading the world into nuclear destruction, Philip Wylie's medusas hiding inside the deceptively reassuring bodies of mom, or Richard Hoggart's dehumanized scholarship boys, cold war social discourses partook of the language of horror to present their particular areas of concern to audiences of the fifties and early sixties. For J. Edgar Hoover, Communists enacted "their evil work" on the unsuspecting (119). In an equal and opposite vein, anti-McCarthyists, like Supreme Court Justice William O. Douglas, labeled McCarthyism as an evil force that "has even entered the univer-

1

sities, great citadels of our spiritual strength and corrupted them" (245). While the language of horror that was used in the anti-communism/anti-McCarthyist debates is what comes to mind most frequently and forcibly when we think of cold war monsters, this discourse of demonization pervaded many levels of social commentary during the fifties.

Philip Wylie's evil mom, a popularization of Freud that re-emphasized the dangers of the mind and found its most forceful expression in *Psycho*; the dangerous, rock-and-roll-drugged juvenile delinquent who wrought havoc in good neighborhoods; the mindless drone of *The Lonely Crowd*—these figures all inspired cold war audiences with fear and found overt expression in horror films that sensationally drew on audiences' anxieties regarding the rapid social changes that had occurred since World War II. Fifties horror tells its audience that no place is safe: not the home, not the work world, not the school, not even the movie theater itself. Moreover, frequently in these films the monsters are presented as being of our own making, such as Tony transformed into a werewolf by his psychiatrist in *I Was a Teenage Werewolf*, or Glenn Manning in *The Amazing Colossal Man* transformed into a giant through a nuclear explosion. Fifties horror films display an awareness of the monsters that haunted cold war society, but also an awareness that many of these monsters were ones that members of that society had created themselves.

Yet, most audiences did not and do not want to watch horror films for social commentary. Cold war horror movies could be sexy, breaking taboos that were firmly entrenched in more respectable films from the time period. Baron's Mesiter's sexy brides in *The Brides of Dracula*; Becky wearing a strapless gown in the middle of the day as she visits Miles Bennell in his office in *Invasion of the Body Snatchers*; Lisa and her lamian seduction in *Cult of the Cobra*—these examples and others point to a strong strain of eroticism in cold war horror films. While the erotic as a component of the horror genre is a commonplace in criticism, in this study, I implicate a particular theorist of the erotic, Georges Bataille, in order to highlight the complex eroticism that exists in both A and B horror film alike.[2] Bataille argues that "Eroticism is the brink of the abyss. I'm leaning out over deranged horror (at this point my eyes roll back in my head). The abyss is the foundation of the possible. We're brought to the edge of the same abyss by uncontrolled laughter or ecstasy. From this comes a questioning of everything possible. This is the stage of rupture, of letting go of things, of looking forward to death" (*Guilty* 109). Bataille's theoretical works shed light on both the universal quality of love and death that is part of the horror genre and the specifics of how cold war angst came to infiltrate the representation of the erotic and intimate.

My purpose in this study is to discuss the social concerns of the cold war in tandem with the erotic and personal. Horror films of the cold war have long been read as allegories of social concerns of their time. Mark Jancovich's *Rational Fears: American Horror in the 1950s* provides an admirable recent study of the issue. This book, however, will use the theories of Georges Bataille in order to discuss how the personal and the public intermingled in a wide variety of horror films. Hence, I am choosing to discuss A-films alongside B-horror films, British horror films alongside American ones, and films that might be classified as ones in which horror is predominant alongside those that are hybrids of the genre, i.e., horror/western, horror/sf, horror/family drama, etc.

What Bataille's theory adds to our understanding of cold war horror films is the fear of/desire for continuity that co-exists with the specific social concerns that are raised in the films. In his study of Bataille's theory, Michael Richardson argues that the central dialectic in Bataille's thought is between continuity and discontinuity. As individuals, we are discontinuous beings who must remain isolated in order to exist; yet, simultaneously, such beings desire "to achieve a state of continuity with what is external" to them (37). Thus, we constantly waver between discontinuity and a desire for continuity, a desire that will only be fulfilled at death. What I am suggesting vis-à-vis cold war horror films is that they operate much the same way. On the one hand, the films invoke a continuous universality through the presence of ancient figures such as the vampire; on the other hand, they strive for a discontinuity with regard to their relationship to other horror films by referencing the specificity of the age. The pleasurable anguish that we as viewers feel when watching one of these films results partly from this dialectic.

I have divided this study into four sections, each one devoted to a particular sociologically defined fear and its manifestation in representative fifties horror films. The first part of the study, "Eroticism and Fifties Horror," examines fifties horror films and their turning to the erotic as refuge from contemporary life. Like the burden of Bataille's postwar criticism, fifties horror turned to the erotic as a haven from the stresses of cold war society; however, just as Bataille was, fifties horror films were aware that what appeared like a haven was in many cases merely a quicker than usual pathway to death. The loss of self charted in erotic experience could frequently be as dangerous as communist takeover or nuclear war. As Chapter 1 discusses, *Invasion of the Body Snatchers*, *Vertigo*, and *The Leech Woman* look to the personal as an alternative to a frightening society of conformity and unhappiness, yet in each of these films the personal fails and leads the films' characters to travel a fine line between life and death.

Chapter 2 focuses on Bataille's theory of taboo and transgression and examines how erotic transgression in fifties horror films works to reinforce social taboos. Thus, *The Bad Seed, Psycho,* and *The Fly,* for example, illustrate how horror films of the period used transgression within the realm of the personal to mirror the larger transgressions that made up cold war politics. Disturbingly, these films suggest that the personal only *appears* as transgressive and opposed to the norms of society. Thus, Rhoda's murders mirror her father's involvement in top-secret military maneuvers; André's transgressive experiments that lead to his becoming a fly/human hybrid are performed in the service of cold war military-industrial experimentation; Norman's murdering of innocent, random victims speaks to a society where the fear of random death via nuclear war weighs very heavily on most people's minds.

The second part of the book, "Evil Others," examines how fifties horror films used familiar figures of evil to express fears of the Other, which most typically meant communist society, and how the erotic was implicated in these representations of evil. Chapter 3 traces the use of the vampire in British and American horror, focusing particularly on *The Horror of Dracula, The Brides of Dracula, Curse of the Undead, The Return of Dracula, First Man Into Space,* and *It! The Terror From Beyond Space.* While the British films retain the mythic allure of the vampire associated with earlier films such as *Dracula, Dracula's Daughter,* and *Son of Dracula,* American horror, through a use of the vampire to symbolize communist take-over, makes the figure repulsive and threatening.

Chapter 4 further traces the use of stock horror figures to embody fears of communism. For both American and British horror films, such as *Cult of the Cobra, Man Beast, The Mummy,* and *Curse of the Mummy's Tomb,* the East and its association with Orientalist stereotypes of evil gained new and more intensified resonance in the cold war when both countries were concerned with formerly Western dominated Eastern countries such as India and their possible capitulation to communist influence. Thus, in these films the residual imperial associations of the East are overlain with evil, with new cold war concerns of communism as a juggernaut, an overwhelmingly corruptive force threatening East and West alike.

The third part of the book, "Horror in the Home," examines how the threats to Western society in the cold war were perceived to come from within as well as without. Thus Chapter 5 examines the influence of fifties' society's fears of dehumanization in the work world on fifties horror films, fears expressed in best-selling sociological studies like David Riesman's *The Lonely Crowd* and William Whyte's *The Organi-*

zation Man. The Amazing Colossal Man, Monster on the Campus, and *The Alligator People* construct monsters that embody a cold war fear that the postwar consumer culture was making humans into drones. Thus, the dominant atmosphere of paranoia was expanded by the thought that if the communists didn't take over society and make Americans into worker slaves, corporate America would take care of the job for them, eliminating the personal and the erotic entirely from human experience. *Horrors of the Black Museum* and *X The Unknown* chart the British fear that the postwar loss of empire had created an impersonal world of killers.

Chapter 6 further charts the horrors within the home front, examining *House of Usher, The Tingler, Village of the Damned,* and *Children of the Damned*—films that illustrate that while both American and British films of the period were concerned about the invasion of the home, their fears were expressed differently. The Freudian-based approach of American horror shows that Americans feared horror within the home coming from the human psyche itself and its inability to resolve internal conflicts. British horror focused on a changing class system that in late forties and fifties Britain threatened to infect the working-class home with a new species known as the scholarship boy.

Part Four, "Teenagers, Moms, and Other Monsters" explores further fears expressed in fifties horror that people living in the same house with the viewer might mutate into something monstrous. Chapter 7 examines teen-themed horror films *The Giant Gila Monster, I Was a Teenage Werewolf,* and *The Blob,* reading them as answers to fifties hysteria concerning juvenile delinquency. While the media frequently portrayed teens as a monstrous threat to the stability of American society, these films show the teen as monster to be a creation of a corrupt adult world.

If the teenager is vindicated in many horror films, mom does not come off so well. Chapter 8 focuses on Philip Wylie's concept of Momism and how it found expression in fifties horror films. In many ways the ultimate fear of cold war sociology was that the enemy could be found in Mom, and that she held undue influence over the coming generations. *House of Wax, The Astounding She-Monster, Phantom of the Rue Morgue,* and "Morella" all chart the fear that in cold war society the feminine could be as degenerative an influence as communism.

Fifties horror films, far from being escapist, charted in their own way many of the major sociological concerns of fifties society. Further, they did so by making the concerns pleasurable, by violating social taboos, using erotic images, and playing on primal fears and desires. By creating a Bataillian world in which the erotic and the terrifying intermingled, these films captured the imaginations of contemporary viewers and later horror afficianados as well. The monsters of the cold war horror film may be identical in form to earlier monsters—Lamia, vampire, werewolf, mummy, all haunt fifties horror films—yet beneath the familiar surface of these age-old myths, much nastier figures could be seen lurking: communists, juvenile delinquents, Moms, or other figures who brought terror into the hearts of cold war American and British society.

Part 1

Eroticism and Fifties Horror

1

ANGUISH:
BATAILLE, EROTICISM, AND FIFTIES HORROR FILMS

Horror films of the 1950s framed the fascination with Liebestod of their Gothic predecessors within the new anxieties of the atomic age. The danger of eroticism and the danger of nuclear war are both played out in these films and their fantasies of identity, love, and death. One twentieth-century thinker who helps shed light on the mechanism of 1950s horror films is Georges Bataille. Ken Hollings argues that for Bataille eroticism is "a surrendering of the self to fear" (206). For an age saturated with the fear of imminent nuclear war, horror provided a means to come face to face with fear via a detour through eroticism. In this chapter I examine three 1950s horror films—*Invasion of the Body Snatchers*, *Vertigo*, and *The Leech Woman*—in order to explore eroticism, death, love, and anguish in the atomic age. These three films represent the prevalence of love, death, and identity as issues in B-films aimed at a teen audience (*Body Snatchers* and *Leech Woman*) and in an A-studio film (*Vertigo*).

For Georges Bataille eroticism is a state that mediates between life and death. In the mediation produced by eroticism the human understands the true basis of his or her subjectivity. Bataille maintains that subjectivity lies in the splits, the wounds of our experience. As Jean Dragon comments, for Bataille "humanity is thus the impossibility of being . . . complete" (44; ellipsis in original). Only in the state of eroticism do human subjects know themselves. In *Guilty* Bataille comments, "Desire for a woman's body, for a tender, erotically naked woman . . . When I'm feeling such pangs of lust, I know best what I am. A sort of hallucinatory darkness pushes me slowly over the edge towards craziness and I start twisting towards impossibility" (12-13). In the loss of identity Bataille experiences in eroticism he finds out what the truth of human subjectivity is.

Bataille argues that the fundamental experience for humanity is anguish. Anguish involves the recognition of our existence as discontinuous beings and simultaneously expresses our desire to find a lost continuity, one that we will find only in death. Anguish is found in the experience of eroticism. As Michael Richardson argues, anguish is a double-edged sword:

As Bataille defined it, anguish is 'the sentiment of danger connected to the inextinguishable expectation.' This sense of anguish is thus at once a sense of loss and profusion. It is present within us not as a negative weight that bears down on us, but as an urge to go beyond our limits, for it is the sense of limits that defines our existence whilst at the same time being connected with the nakedness of existence, a nakedness that for Bataille was rending and painful. (37)

Bataille's theories of the erotic and subjectivity are suggestive for reading 1950s horror not because they offer a universal key to understanding human experience but because Bataille's theories, like the films under discussion, are symptomatic of the stresses of World War II and the ensuing cold war. Bataille perceives the experience of eroticism to be something outside of history. In *The Accursed Share* Bataille states that "individual love . . . is the least historical thing in the world. It is not an aspect of history, and if it depends on historical conditions this is to a small extent" (Vol. II., 157). Yet Bataille's discussions of eroticism after World War II are frequently framed within reference to nuclear weapons. Bataille compares the loss of self and release of energy found in the erotic act to the atomic bomb, commenting that "On this scale, the chain releases of atomic energy are nothing" (*Accursed*, Vol. II, 183-84). Bataille further argues that the excess energy not spent in eroticism in society will find expression in the holocaust of total war (*Accursed* 188). As Richardson notes, Bataille believes that capitalism, with its denial of expenditure, a quality he sees at the base of eroticism, channels energy into catastrophe instead of the erotic. In capitalism energy takes the shape of war, killings, and nuclear explosion, forms of expression of energy that Bataille believes are fundamental to the structure of capitalism (94).

Thus Bataille sets up the erotic in opposition to nuclear war. While the erotic shows our desire to return to a state of continuity present in death it seems to be a possible panacea to nuclear war, where the desire to return to the continuity present in death is writ large in global destruction. The fantasy of erotic experience as a counter to world catastrophe found in Bataille's writings is also present in the three films under discussion here. Like Bataille's works, these films suggest a universality in the experience of eroticism. In *Erotism: Death and Sensuality*, Bataille states, "It is always at bottom a matter of two incompatibles: the realm of calm and rational behavior and the violence of the sexual impulse" (53). Bataille's desire to posit a universal theory of eroticism in the face of a radically changing world is a desire well understood by 1950s horror films.

Invasion of the Body Snatchers (1956), a film that spans the science-fiction and horror categories, directly offers eroticism as a means of countering the horror of a conformist society represented by the replicants who gradually take over Santa Mira.[1] The film is narrated by Miles Bennell, a medical doctor who returns home because people have been demanding his services. He finds a town in which people are convinced that their closest relatives have been replaced by imposters. Teaming up with the newly divorced Becky Driscoll, Miles' former college sweetheart, Miles becomes embroiled in a mystery. At his friends the Bellicecs' house he and Becky witness a strange, unformed body. Miles then discovers a replicant of Becky in her father's basement. While the police and a psychiatrist attempt to convince Miles he is delusional, he and Becky and the Bellicecs see the reality of the threat when they discover seed pods giving birth to replicants of their bodies in a greenhouse. Miles and Becky attempt to leave town, but are stopped. They hide in Miles' office, finally running from the replicants and hiding in a tunnel. Miles leaves Becky to seek help, but she transforms. Miles then flees to the highway where he is picked up and taken to a mental ward. When an accident involving one of the trucks carrying the seedpods is reported, the authorities believe Miles' story and call in the FBI.

Many critics have placed the film firmly within the context of atomic age fears.[2] Most blatantly, however, the film focuses on the personal, with eroticism and love being lauded as the only defenses against the invasion.[3] Siegel maintained that his idea in making the film was to warn against the loss of humanity in everyday life. In an interview he stated, "Pods. Not those that come from outer space, vegetables from outer space. People are pods. Many of my associates are certainly pods. They have no feelings. They exist, breathe, sleep. To be a pod means that you have no passion, no anger, the spark has left you" (qtd. In Kaminsky 154). As Bataille locates humanity in the experience of the erotic, so does Siegel's film. Miles' growing awareness of the presence of the pods parallels his growing sexual attraction to Becky. As Miles learns from his secretary, Sally, why he has been called back early from the conference, his interest is peaked more by her mentioning the fact that Becky has returned from London than her mentioning the facts surrounding the large number of patients who demand to see him. When Becky arrives at Miles' office to relate the strange behavior of her cousin Wilma, she is the very image of erotic beauty, dressed in a strapless sundress and flirting with Miles. Initially the burgeoning romance between Becky and Miles serves as comic relief to the eerie world of the replicants. As

Becky and Miles go to a restaurant together, prior to their discovery of the body at the Bellicecs' house, they kiss, and Becky asks Miles if this behavior is an example of his bedside manner, to which he replies, "No, ma'am, that comes later" (48). Jack Finney's novel, on which the film is based, is even more explicit in its use of the erotic as a counterpart to the mystery of the pods. After rescuing Becky from an imminent transformation, Miles thinks two thoughts at the same time: "*They're going to get us*, I thought lifting my head to stare at Jack, and at the same time—*Now, Becky has to stay here*" (100).[4] If the erotic attraction between Becky and Miles is initially a powerful but hesitant one because both of them have recently been divorced, it evolves into the signifier for their humanity.

As Miles and Becky fall deeply in love, their anguish increases. The flirtation with madness that Bataille links with eroticism and the experience of anguish is central to Miles' experience in the film. Early in the action Miles attempts to reassure Wilma that her uncle Ira hasn't changed by telling her, "Even these days it isn't as easy to go crazy as you might think" (45). Yet, go crazy is just what Miles must do in order to remain a human. The Miles of the film's frame is the very picture of anguish, and the doctors perceive him as insane.[5] Earlier in the film when Miles makes a pass at Becky in her hallway, she responds by saying, "That way lies madness" (55). Yet, like Miles, she will embrace madness, the madness of her love for Miles, as the sign of her difference from the pod people. Unlike Miles, Becky will transform. She will make the transition from eroticism to madness to a state of continuity very like death, an existence as a pod person. Curiously, it is after Becky and Miles metaphorically experience both sex and death that Becky transforms. Pursued by the replicants, Becky and Miles hide themselves under wooden boards in a tomblike structure. Inside the refuge, they hide in a sexual embrace. During the postcoital cleaning, as they wash themselves with water from a small pool in the tunnel, Miles hears music and leaves Becky to her transformation. Thus, while if Miles remains in a state of anguish, Becky gives in to the dream of continuity represented by pod society.[6]

While the pods initially appear to be opposed to the eroticism of Becky and Miles, they are, in fact, intimately connected to it. The pods represent the natural world, the continuity of nature, and death. Richardson comments that for Bataille, "The denial of eroticism . . . is at the same time an attempt to deny and close out death and our connection with nature" (104). Giving in to the pod society might be read as a giving in to nature and death: for Becky this is the course taken and one that is taken through eroticism. Bataille comments that "anguish, which lays us open to annihilation and death, is always linked to eroticism; our sexual activity finally rivets us to the distressing image of death, and the knowledge of death deepens the abyss of eroticism." (*Accursed*, Vol. II., 84). What distinguishes Becky and Miles is that Miles does not give in to death but remains on the edge of the abyss, in the state of anguish. Miles' most intense moment in the film is when he discovers that Becky has transformed: "I've been afraid a lot of times in my life, but I didn't know the real meaning of fear until . . . until I kissed Becky" (103; ellipsis in original). The anguish lies in the fact that in her transformed face he has glimpsed his own desire for the continuity of death.

As Bataille locates in eroticism the paradox that in what we consider the most personal state and act—love—is housed a means to loss of identity, a means to the impersonal, so Siegel's film makes the same connection. Bataille states that "there is such a feeling of intoxication when we find love . . . When love is another planet, we collapse in it, free of the emptiness of our strumming and unhappiness. In fact, in love we stop being ourselves" (*Guilty* 111). In relation to a film concerned primarily with the loss of self, this is a suggestive statement. Giving in to the pod society is one way to lose self in the film, yet Miles also loses self due to his love for Becky and then to his loss of her. While he does not become the emotionless human Becky does, he becomes the madman, raving, stopping traffic, and almost being confined to an institution. In the film's frame his attempts to try to re-establish his old identity are unsuccessful. In the beginning sequence of the film Miles pleads with Dr. Hill, a psychiatrist, stating, "I'm a doctor too. I am not insane! I am not insane!" (32). Miles tries to assert his authority, but cannot. Even after hearing the entire story, Dr. Hill still believes Miles is "Mad as a March hare" (107). Although Miles is finally believed when a truck accident involving a load of pods fortuitously reveals the truth to others, the last image we see of Miles is one of anguish, one of madness as he "grits his teeth into a half-smile" (109).

Siegel's film problematically deals with the attempt on the part of 1950s society to pose eroticism as a defense against a process of dehumanization occurring due to nuclear weapons and the escalating cold war. Lewis Mumford, for example, emphasizes the personal, i.e., love, as an antidote to a dehumanized and dehumanizing society bent on nuclear destruction (60-61). In *The Lonely Crowd*, David Riesman also sees the erotic as a possible way to break with the conformity he diagnoses in a society gradually transforming into other-directed men. He sees sexuality as "a kind of defense against the threat of total apathy" (154). For Riesman, this turning toward sex on the part of the other-directed man is a futile attempt to find "reassurance that he is still alive" (15). Thus, although Miles' love for Becky removes him from total apathy, it doesn't take him as far away from the deathlike pod world as we might imagine. Yet, Miles' ability to embrace eroticism and its state of anguish leaves him in a state of suspension, between sanity and insanity, between the pod world and the human world. The film leaves him in an unresolved position.

A more famous film protagonist begins his journey into anguish literally in a state of suspension. Scottie Ferguson of *Vertigo* (1958) dangles between life and death at the opening of the film and remains metaphorically suspended there for the rest of the film.[7] *Vertigo* focuses on Scottie Ferguson, an ex-police detective who is unable to work because of vertigo, a condition he discovers he suffers from as he and a policeman chase a criminal on a San Francisco rooftop. The policeman dies trying to save Scottie. Galvin Elster, a college friend of Scottie's, contacts him and asks him to follow his wife, Madeleine. Elster states that he believes the spirit of her dead ancestor Carlotta Valdes has possessed her. Scottie follows her and falls in love with her, trying to save her until she apparently jumps to her death from the belltower at the Mission San Juan Bautista. Scottie suffers a mental breakdown and is hospitalized. After being released he searches for Madeleine, finally finding Judy, a woman who resembles her. The audience discovers that Judy and Madeleine are the same woman. This is revealed in a letter Judy writes disclosing that she played Madeleine in a plot to kill the real Madeleine and use Scottie as a credible witness to a suicide. Judy tears up the letter. Scottie begins a process of transforming her into Madeleine. When the physical transformation is complete Judy puts on a necklace that resembles the necklace Carlotta wears in her portrait, and Scottie realizes he has been tricked. He forces Judy to return to San Juan Bautista, and she jumps to death when a nun frightens her.

There are very clear connections we can make between Hitchcock's film and the horror genre. Kim Newman argues that in the twentieth century, "horror becomes less like a discrete genre than an effect which can be deployed with any number of settings or narrative patterns, burrowing like a parasite" into other genres (11). Thus, Newman includes an entry on Hitchcock in her *BFI Companion to Horror* citing Hitchcock's fascination "with abnormal psychological states" (156). Nowhere does this fascination stand out more clearly than in *Vertigo*. S. S. Prawer argues that Hitchcock's films typically demonstrate the fluidity between the suspense-thriller genre and the horror film (17). David Hogan suggests that although Hitchcock "did not make his fortune and reputation with movies about monsters and headless ghosts . . . his films inarguably deal with the horrors of the mind: with guilt, paranoia, and sexual insanity" (182). *Vertigo* has a very intimate connection to the horror genre because, unlike most of Hitchcock's films, it invokes the supernatural and never entirely explains it away.[8] Hitchcock's further connection to horror can be found in the influence Edgar Allan Poe exerted on his work. In an essay titled "Why I am Afraid of the Dark," Hitchcock cited Poe as a formative influence on his films, stating that he and Poe both worked by creating "a completely unbelievable story told to the readers [or viewers] with such a spellbinding logic that you get the impression that the same thing could happen to you tomorrow" (qtd. in Wollen 17).[9] Thus, while *Vertigo* would not have played on a double bill with *Invasion of the Body Snatchers* or *The Leech Woman*, its concerns are similar to the concerns of these more obvious horror films.

Much of the criticism of Hitchcock's film has centered on how Scottie, through his obsessive idealization of Woman, ends up destroying Judy. Critics have seen his actions as symptomatic of masculine desire in a patriarchal culture.[10] While this criticism has yielded very fruitful discussion of the film, I want to approach the issue of the erotic from a different angle. Marian E. Keane suggests that what *Vertigo* reveals to us is not so much the brutality of the male gaze, à la Laura Mulvey, but something more disturbing: "What is shown to be brutal in *Vertigo* is the nature of human desire and need, not some function of a particular phase of male development whose correction it is fairly simple to imagine" (236). I, too, believe that the film is revealing a fantasy of eroticism that is more than just a masculine fantasy. Bataille's disturbing dream of eroticism has much in common with Hitchcock's dream and both implicate male and female subjects in the fantasy.

Bataille makes an opposition between eroticism and the world of work. He argues that one reason eroticism troubles contemporary society is because capitalistic society has been predicated on acquisition, whereas the act of eroticism is predicated on a reckless expenditure. Tracing the attempt to control eroticism back to ancient taboos, Bataille concludes that violence, which he sees as part of the experience of eroticism, is the element the world of work tries to keep at bay with strict taboos (*Erotism* 42). Because as humans we "stand abashed in front of death or sexual union" society attempts to exclude these experiences through prohibitions (*Erotism* 50). Modern capitalistic society has a special stake in making the erotic taboo because eroticism is an anti-acquisitive state: "If we follow the dictates of reason we try to acquire all kinds of goods . . . But when the fever of sex seizes us we behave in the opposite way. We recklessly draw our strength and sometimes in the violence of passion we squander considerable resources to no real purpose" (*Erotism* 170). The very uselessness of eroticism troubles a society predicated on utilitarianism and consumerism.

Thus, while Bataille posits the erotic as universally opposed to the world of work, this opposition is part of a central debate during the 1950s. Works such as *The Lonely Crowd, The Man in the Gray Flannel Suit, From the Terrace,* and others attest to a growing concern in the 1950s that the world of work was encroaching on the personal and robbing the individual of his humanity. David Halberstam discusses the significant impact both the novel and film versions of *The Man in the Gray Flannel* suit had on American culture because the story tapped into a significant debate for mid-1950s society: "The debate seemed to focus on the question of whether, despite the significant and dramatic increase in the standard of living for many Americans, the new white-collar life was turning into something of a trap and whether the greater material benefits it promised and delivered were being exchanged for freedom and individuality" (527). Bataille's move of opposing the world of work with the world of eroticism has similarities with 1950s America's desire to set in contrast the corporate world and freedom. Yet, as I will discuss below, Bataille complicates this notion, as *Vertigo* does, by suggesting that what is sought in the personal realm is ultimately not individuality but an obliteration of the individual.

Vertigo establishes an opposition between the world of work and the world of eroticism from the very beginning. One of Midge's functions in the film is to embody the world of work and its supposed virtues. Some critics have seen her as the indicator of a normality in the film, an antidote to obsession, but it is difficult for me to see that the film is endorsing her position.[11] In the first sequence that follows Scottie's near-death experience on the roof, Midge implicitly scolds Scottie because he refuses to go back to work. She refuses to go out for a beer with him because she is busy working on a new bra design. While Midge works in an ostensibly erotic field—underwear design—it has been completely assimilated into consumerism. She is interested in bras because people buy them, not because they are one of the last objects of clothing taken off during erotic encounters.[12] Other characters linked with the world of work are also set in opposition to both Scottie and Madeleine. During Scottie's first meeting with Galvin Elster, Elster casts himself as the man whose life has been taken over by the corporate world. He has married into the shipping business and has responsibilities that prevent him from following Madeleine to discover the cause of her strange behavior. Even though Elster's argument is merely a ruse to trap Scottie, the film suggests to us that the logic of Elster's corporate world leads to calculated manipulation and murder. After Madeleine's apparent death the coroner at the inquest also embodies the world of work, scolding Scottie for his reckless behavior in allowing Madeleine to throw herself from the tower.

The world of Scottie and Madeleine, and then its repetition in the world of Scottie and Judy, is one of reckless expenditure. It is Scottie's status as someone who no longer works that allows him to become embroiled in Elster's plot. During their first meeting, Elster tells Scottie that Madeleine "wanders," a word that is taken up again and again in both the visual images and dialogue of the film. After Madeleine throws herself into San Francisco Bay and Scottie rescues her, they both identify themselves as people with no occupation, wanderers. Madeleine says she was "wandering about." Scottie takes up the phrase and tells her that his profession is "wandering about." The next day when Madeleine goes to Scottie's apartment to apologize, Scottie asks if they can wander together, to which Madeleine replies, "only one is a wanderer. Two are always going somewhere." Scottie disagrees with this. The growing erotic attraction between Scottie and Madeleine is the product of their ability to reject the world of work and wander aimlessly. Later, when Scottie finds Judy he persuades her to call in sick to work in order to spend time with him, aimlessly wandering through the city. It is only when Scottie reclaims the work world, as detective again, and not lover, as he drags Judy up the stairs of the Mission San Juan Bautista, "We're going up and looking at the scene of the crime," that Judy jumps to her death.

Vertigo shows us that rejecting the world of work and giving in to erotic wastefulness is a state that houses the desire to obliterate identity. Rejecting the world of work does not lead to finding one's individuality, but, rather, is predicated on a desire to give in to continuity, to give up the burden of personality. Scottie is erotically drawn to Madeleine because of her loss of personality. In the first meeting with Elster, Scottie becomes intrigued when Elster tells him that Madeleine is "someone I didn't know." Scottie's first glimpse of Madeleine that draws him to her is a statue-like pose as the camera frames her in profile. In the Redwoods sequence Scottie becomes further drawn to Madeleine because her own personality disappears. "Madeleine, where are you now?" he asks her. During this sequence Madeleine and Scottie kiss for the first time, Scottie drawn to her apparent state of possession, of lost, or displaced personality. In Pierre Boileau's and Thomas Narcejac's novel *D'entre Les Morts* (Translated as *The Living and the Dead*) on which the film is based. Flavières (the model for Scottie) first becomes erotically attracted to Madeleine when he watches her at the opera, seeing in her physical appearance, "the face of a statue, the eyes hardly bringing it to life at all" (38).

For Bataille, what is erotically attractive and frightening in the beloved is not personality, but the absence of it that occurs in the sexual act. Bataille argues that in the erotic act a man and a woman no longer see each other as individuals (*Guilty* 31). Bataille says that desire "always seeks two objects, one that is mobile and alive, another that is fixated and dead. And what characterizes eroticism is not the mobile-living, but the fixed-dead, which alone is detached from the normal world" (*Accursed*, Vol. II 143). Scottie is drawn to the fixed-dead image of Madeleine as statue, as woman possessed by a dead relative. Her statue-like features and trances invoke for him the power of the erotic act to obliterate personality. Bataille discusses the shock at seeing the dignified woman engaged in passionate lovemaking, arguing that it appears to be an act of madness because "for the time being the personality is dead" (*Erotism* 106). Madeleine's loss of identity present in her perfect appearance and possessed mind invoke, thus, not the ethereal woman but the woman in the throes of passion. Scottie's attraction to Madeleine is hence not so much to the idealized woman but to the woman lost to erotic activity.[13] Scottie is drawn to Madeleine's loss of personality because that is what he longs for too: the obliteration of the self in erotic engulfment.[14]

Yet the film does not deal only with the male subject's desire to lose identity. The focus on Judy in the latter part of the film shows us that she, too, houses a desire to give up her personality to Scottie by becoming Madeleine again. Judy hovers between wanting to cling to her identity and longing to sacrifice it to Scottie's erotic dream. When Judy tears up the confession letter, she starts the course of repeating the loss of identity she already experienced in her relationship with Elster. Bathed in the green light of the Empire Hotel and shot in profile, Judy agrees to not go to work the next day, assenting to Scottie's plan to remake her into Madeleine. Judy finds herself in a state of anguish as she battles impulses to cling to herself as Judy and impulses that propel her to becoming Madeleine, the site of loss of personality. When she agrees to change her appearance she tells Scottie, "I'll do it. I don't care anymore about me." Yet, even after the physical transformation she still resists completely giving herself up to Madeleine. She does not fix her hair in the proper manner, but when she emerges from the bathroom with it pinned up, she is bathed in the green light. The erotic engulfs both Scottie and Madeleine at that point, and they make love for perhaps the first time.[15]

As in *Invasion of the Body Snatchers* it is after both the characters have given in to eroticism that a veering towards death occurs, and, as in the earlier film, it is the woman who succumbs to the fantasy of continuity. Judy's anguish finally leads her to leap from the tower. Like Becky she is unable to exist in the in-between state, hovering between life and death, sanity and insanity. Scottie, however, like Miles, remains perpetually suspended. Bataille argues that when in a state of desire the lover wants that which exhausts him or her and even that which endangers his or her life (*Accursed*, Vol. II, 104). In *The Living and the Dead* Flavières' love for Madeleine is described in the following terms: "She absorbed literally all his strength. He was a blood-donor. No, that wasn't the word. A soul-donor" (63). Scottie comes close to death because of his love for Madeleine, as the scenes in which a catatonic Scottie in the asylum cannot communicate with Midge, and, more obviously, as Scottie's dream of death demonstrate. Yet, at the end of the film Scottie is not dead. In the state of suspension Scottie begins and ends in, he embodies Bataille's truly alive human, the one who can stand at the edge of the abyss, but not succumb to it. Richardson describes the state of the human in Bataille's theory thus: "our essential motivation (motivated, that is, by anguish) is to go beyond our limits and yet, at the same time, it is apparent that if we were to do so we would in fact cease to exist. The most we can do, therefore, is to experience the vertigo at the edge on which our life unfolds" (38). For Bataille the man who understands his humanity is the one who is in a state of vertigo. Bataille explicitly addresses the issue of vertigo, stating that the lover "should not succumb to vertigo . . . he alone is happy who, having experienced vertigo to the point of trembling in his bones, to the point of being incapable of measuring the extent of his fall, suddenly finds the unhoped-for strength to turn his agony into a joy" (*Visions* 235-36). Though it seems unlikely that Scottie will be able to turn his vertigo into anything positive at the end of the film—Scottie's dream and the movie poster for the film suggest that Scottie's next act will be to throw himself on Judy's body—the film chooses to leave him in the state of vertigo, not having succumbed to it as Judy has.[16]

The most obvious explanation as to why both Becky and Judy must give in to continuity, and Miles and Scottie remain suspended is that both films are told from the perspective of the male protagonist. The death of the woman in both films also relates to her status as the beautiful woman who through her erotic attractiveness leads the lover to a confrontation with death. Bataille was fascinated with the eye as a symbol. His novel *The Story of the Eye* makes much of this motif. In an essay entitled "Eye" Bataille theorizes why the fear of the eye has been prominent in human history: "It seems impossible, in fact, to judge the eye using any word other than *seductive*, since nothing is more attractive in the bodies of animals and men. But extreme seductiveness is probably at the boundary of horror" (*Visions* 17; emphasis in original). Bataille could be describing Saul Bass' famous opening credits sequence for *Vertigo*, as woman's eye serves as the progenitor for the seductiveness and horror of the film itself. Scottie's attraction for Madeleine's beauty is one that straddles the boundary between seductiveness and horror.

Bataille theorizes that the lover's desire for the beautiful woman is more intense because it suspends him between beauty and violence. Bataille argues that eroticism motivates the lover to break taboos and spoil beauty (*Erotism* 145). Thus, in the contradiction between the poised beautiful woman and her abandon in the sexual act, eroticism is born. In François Truffaut's famous interviews with Hitchcock, Hitchcock discusses his ideal of feminine sexuality as one that sustains these types of contrasts: "Sex should not be advertised. An English girl, looking like a schoolteacher, is apt to get into a cab with you and, to your surprise, she'll probably pull a man's pants open" (224). Madeleine's great beauty draws Scottie to her because his erotic desire longs to despoil her, revealing beneath the individual woman, a link to the continuous process of death. Scottie falls in love with Madeleine after he saves her from drowning and undresses her. Having glimpsed her nudity, he is more than just interested in her, he is obsessed with her, in love with her. Discussing Bataille's views of nudity, Hollings argues that "True nakedness is a confrontation with the charnel house of the body: the knowledge of physical mortality and frailty" (203-04). Having seen Madeleine's body, Scottie has seen the decay of the beautiful woman, and, by implication, his own decay.

Thus, like Bataille and like *Invasion of the Body Snatchers*, *Vertigo* opposes eroticism to the world of work, the world of conformity and consumerism that threatens to rob people of their humanity. Yet, the paradox lies in the fact that in the act of being most human, falling in love, succumbing to erotic desire, the human is threatened with the loss of self and the loss of life. The apocalyptic overtones of a postwar embracing of the personal show a connection to the engulfment of nuclear holocaust. Overlaid onto the age-old Liebestod motif is an urgency to seek annihilation in the personal realm of eroticism before the world annihilates itself. While *Body Snatchers* and *Vertigo* suggest that this fantasy plays out only when the woman herself succumbs to death while the man hovers over it, the last film under discussion here illustrates that the fantasy may not be an exclusively masculine one.

The Leech Woman (1959) focuses on June Talbot, a neglected and aging doctor's wife, who has fallen into alcoholism because of her husband's cruel treatment of her. Her husband, Paul, shows renewed interest in her after meeting Mala, a 140-year-old member of a secret African tribe, who tells him that if he will travel to Africa, she will show him the secret of restoring youth. Paul tricks June into going along with him to Africa because he wants to use her as a guinea pig. At the ceremony at which Mala is transformed into a young woman again she offers June the same opportunity. The transformation requires the blood of a man in order to succeed and June chooses Paul as her victim. She then must kill regularly in order to stay young. Back in Los Angeles she kills a con man and her attorney's fiancée and eventually is caught up with by the police. She jumps from the window and dies before she can be captured.

While this relatively unknown B-film has not been accorded the critical prestige that both *Body Snatchers* and *Vertigo* have, it engages many of the same issues that they do and, by adopting a feminine perspective, indicates the same processes of eroticism at work in the masculine-perspective of the previously discussed films. The film indicates the closeness between erotic desire and self-destructiveness. If both Miles and Scottie skirt madness due to their erotic desire, June battles alcoholism. At the beginning of the film as we see her desperate attempts to get attention from a husband who considers her to be repulsive, she says to Paul, "drinking, my feelings for you are both bad for me." She agrees to grant Paul a divorce, but Mala stops her as she leaves Paul's office and tells her, "You are the one in my dreams of blood," promising her that "You will never divorce your husband. He will die." Mala's foretelling of Paul's death disturbs June, but Mala is speaking her desire. At the ceremony in which Mala is transformed into a young woman, June chooses to sacrifice Paul so she can regain youth and be erotically attractive again. She makes this decision because Paul has threatened to sacrifice her life so he can escape from the mysterious tribe.

Bataille makes an explicit link between eroticism and sacrifice: "Eroticism is analogous to a tragedy, where the hecatomb at the end brings together all the characters. The point is that the totality reached (yet indefinitely out of reach) is reached only at the price of sacrifice: eroticism reaches it precisely inasmuch as love is a kind of immolation" (*Accursed*, Vol. II, 119). June realizes a truth about eroticism when she sacrifices Paul instead of allowing him to sacrifice her. Earlier June has pleaded with Paul to love her, telling him, "I'd even die for you." But, it is Paul's death that makes June's experience of anguish possible as she hovers between youth (in her new identity as Terry Hart) and approaching death (in her old identity as the rapidly aging June Talbot). Here it is the man who must succumb to the continuity of death in order to make the experience of anguish possible.

The film also parallels Bataille's idea of eroticism being possible only in regard to a beautiful woman. Paul, David (the guide in Africa), and Neil Foster (June's attorney) are all find themselves repelled by June when she is old. Paul shoves her away as she tries to take his arm. David pushes her to the ground, horrified, when he sees that she has changed from a beautiful, young woman, into a rapidly aging one. Bataille argues that the beautiful woman alone provokes erotic desire because she allows for no contrast between physical beauty and the ugliness of the genitals (*Erotism* 145). June's transformations play out that contrast. She is not attractive when she is merely old, but she has enhanced attractiveness when she exists in a state hovering between a horrific, aging, decaying body and a beautiful young woman. This fact is attested to when she makes love with the guide immediately after they escape from Mala, and later as she is able to seduce Neil while his fiancée is waiting in the car.

What makes her attractive, then, is her heightened connection with death. Mala has warned June that the youthfulness can last only a brief period of time, and then she must die. Every time June transforms back she becomes older, closer to a corpse, and this heightens her beauty after she has taken the potion again. Further, it is the erotic sacrifice of men that makes her beauty possible. Her next victim after Paul is David, whom she kills while pretending to save him from quicksand. The third victim is a con man, who is pretending to seduce her in order to steal her jewels. June's fatal mistake occurs when she kills Sally, Neil's fiancée, and drinks her blood mixed with the potion. This act causes her to age further, and she throws herself out the window, horrified that she can no longer be young. The film suggests that only through dead men— through what are for June dead objects of desire—is the state of erotic anguish possible. A woman's blood does not work because there is no erotic connection between the two women. Thus, the fantasy of suspension between life and death over the dead beloved we saw in the two earlier films follows a similar pattern here with the exception that it is dead men, not dead women, that make the state of anguish possible.

The fantasy of the erotic as a refuge from the world of work is, perhaps, a postwar feminine fantasy as much as it is a postwar masculine fantasy. While *The Leech Woman* is not a film made by women, many 1950s women could easily identify with a character who has lost her value due to losing her youth. Mala explicitly voices this idea at the ceremony when she says, "For a man old age has rewards," but "the aged woman is nothing." Here she is speaking June's feelings and presumably the feelings of many women in 1950s society. What I am suggesting is that the fantasy of the erotic as complicated and dangerous refuge from the stresses of the atomic age is one that crosses gender lines.

It is, further, one that suggests that in an uncertain age of possible nuclear war, the refuge itself is merely a fine line away from annihilation. As Bataille sees it, in the wartorn twentieth century the only place left to experience the anguish of what it means to be human is eroticism: "The lost, the tragic, the 'blinding marvel,' possessed in one's innermost being, can no longer be met anywhere but on a bed. It is true that satisfied lust and the dissociated concerns of the present world also invade bedrooms; locked bedrooms nevertheless remain, in the almost unlimited mental void, so many islands where the images of life reconstitute themselves" (*Visions* 228). Bataille's complicated vision of eroticism and what it means to pre- and post-war Western society hence found a common expression in these very different 1950s horror films. In a society faced with fears of dehumanization and annihilation the horror of the erotic experience stood as a dark counterpart to a world apparently on the verge of self-destruction. Eroticism as an act of transgression within the cold war world of taboos remains another way in which it informed fifties horror films.

2

TABOO AND TRANSGRESSION
IN *THE BAD SEED, THE FLY,* AND *PSYCHO*

An eight-year-old girl commits three cold-blooded murders. Through reckless experimentation a scientist fuses his body with a fly's. A young man keeps his mother's dead body in his house. The horror film is a genre that operates within a framework of taboo and transgression. Following its Gothic predecessors it expresses the most serious of transgressions— murder, necrophilia, incest, etc.—highlighting the taboo that prohibits such activities. The cold war period in American history was an age when taboo and transgression became highlighted. As taboos were emphasized more and more in 1950s America the allure of transgression was heightened. One place the interplay between taboo and transgression was expressed was in the horror film. By reading three very different film manifestations of 1950s horror through the theories of Georges Bataille, this analysis articulates the interplay of taboo and transgression in three horror films from the cold war period: *The Bad Seed, The Fly,* and *Psycho.*

In Bataille's works transgression is a desire created by the taboo itself. Discussing sexual transgression Bataille comments that prohibition against sexual objects drew attention to the allure of those objects (*Accursed* II, 48). The taboo gives the transgression a value it would not possess outside of its relationship to the taboo. In making a distinction with the animal world Bataille argues that transgression is something unique to human existence because of human society's creation of taboos. Taboos help to maintain order in society, but they also provide a space for transgression to develop. Bataille states that taboo makes violence forbidden, but simultaneously provides a possibility for violence to erupt (*Accursed* II, 57). The limits imposed by the taboo make the transgressive act one that is appealing. Thus, "The limits give passion the contracted movement that it did not have in animality" (*Accursed* III, 221). Thus transgression is never a simple reversion to animality, but is something that is uniquely human. As Bataille sees it fear and horror are emotional states that inspire the act of transgression. He comments that the emotional states of fear and horror provide a temptation, a catalyst, for transgressive behavior (*Erotism* 144). It is the experience of terror that allows the transgression to accrue value: "the forbidden action takes on a significance it lacks before fear widens the gap between us and it and invests it with an aura of excitement" (*Erotism* 48). Thus in human society as in the horror film it is the experience of fear that gives value to the transgressive act.

Bataille's understanding of taboo and transgression is especially insightful because it does not posit transgression as an act that undermines taboo. Within Bataille's thought transgression never represents a simple subversion of the dominant order. As Michael Richardson observes, in Bataille's writings neither taboo nor transgression holds a privileged place. As concepts, they complete and validate each other (9). Thus while the taboo stands as a limit that makes the act of transgression attractive, so the act of transgression reinforces the power of the taboo. In discussing erotic transgression Bataille comments that "In erotic excess we venerate the rule which we break" (*Literature* 139).

Bataille understands the mutual dependence of taboo and transgression within a larger framework of what he terms the sacred and the profane. As Bataille sees it, the sacred is constituted by transgressive acts: the sacred is constituted by prohibited acts (*Accursed* II, 92). The profane world is the world of taboos, specifically the world of work and reason. In the sacred world the human seeks a lost unity, a continuity that will be found ultimately only in death. For Bataille, the totality one attempts to find in the sacred, a totality that always remains out of reach, is sought for "only at the price of a sacrifice" (*Accursed* II, 119). Within taboo and transgression the interplay between the profane and the sacred is a dangerous one. Bataille argues that humanity on the one hand strives to avoid death and on the other seeks to enhance the intensity of experience. These two goals clash and produce a potentially dangerous situation (*Literature* 73-74).

For Bataille, what constitutes transgression is violence. The transition to different states Bataille perceives in both eroticism and death disturbs the calm world of work with a disruption that recalls a frightening unity. The loss of the self is paramount in both of these experiences. In discussing earlier cultures Bataille argues that all death was perceived as an act of violence, commenting that earlier man always believed there was a murderer responsible for any death that occurred (*Erotism* 47). Transgression is always an act of sacrifice, because it is an attempt to eliminate individuality in favor of continuity beyond the self. The violence of eroticism and the violence of murder are both such transgressive acts: "The lover strips the beloved of her identity no less than the bloodstained priest his animal or human victim" (*Erotism* 90). Bataille's theory provides a means of understanding the disturbing conjunction of eroticism and violence found in horror films like *Psycho*.

In Bataille's writings the interplay between taboo and transgression is increasingly understood within the framework of international politics and ultimately provides a means of understanding the cold war. Jean-Michel Besnier observes that "Taking the form of war, the sacred would in fact threaten man with total annihilation" (24). The invention of nuclear weapons made this scenario a real possibility. As Bataille's friend and colleague Jean Piel comments, Bataille began to perceive the cold war as a means of avoiding the catastrophe of nuclear war. While Bataille feared that the excess energy of the sacred might be spent in war, by the 1950s he "saw clearly that the USSR was there as if to awaken the world, and that America, actually feeling the effect of this permanent threat, began to awaken to an awareness. He had the illumination that 'paradoxical changes' could be established between these two forces and thus prove 'that the contradictions of the world are not necessarily resolved by war'"(105). As Piel notes, Bataille was a "prophet of 'peaceful coexistence' and of unexpected developments of the competition for expansion between the two blocs" (105). Bataille's writing and its emphasis on taboo and transgression, while purporting to formulate a universal theory of these concepts, was firmly grounded in concerns of history. Similarly, 1950s horror films frequently posit universals of human behavior while operating within very specific historical concerns.

The Bad Seed (1956) is a horror film that transgresses the taboo on children as murderers.[1] The film is based on William March's novel of the same name and on a play derived from that novel. *The Bad Seed* concerns Rhoda Penmark, an eight-year-old girl who is on the surface the very epitome of the well-behaved child, but underneath is a psychotic killer. Her mother, Christine, learns the truth about Rhoda while her husband, Kenneth, is away on business. Rhoda kills Claude Daigle, a classmate of hers, in order to steal his penmanship medal, which, she believes, she should have won. Rhoda then kills LeRoy, a handyman who has been teasing her about the Daigle child's death. The film reveals that Rhoda had earlier killed an old woman in order to get a trinket the woman had promised that she would have after her death. Christine, having become suspicious of Rhoda's behavior, delves into her own past, discovering that she has been adopted and that her true mother is Bessie Denker, a psychopathic killer who started her crimes at age ten. Christine believes she has passed the "bad seed" on to Rhoda. Out of guilt she gives Rhoda an overdose of sleeping pills and shoots herself. She and Rhoda both survive, but Rhoda is struck by lightening when she goes to recover the penmanship medal, which Christine has thrown off the wharf.

Controversy surrounding the making of the film highlights its status as transgressive film. Jerold Simmons argues that the Production Code, under Geoffrey Shurlock, objected to a film version of the play *The Bad Seed* because of the fear that it would influence young viewers. As one Production Code reader noted, "The identification of youngsters with Rhoda . . . will be very complete. They will understand her *effective* killing of three persons who stood in her way, while at the same time, since Rhoda is a poised, charming child, they will *completely* miss her psychotic and tragic nature . . . a very dangerous combination" (4). While Shurlock continued to veto approval for the film, Martin Quigley, co-author of the original Production Code, commented on the potential financial success of the film, stating that it was "just enough off-beat to interest today's distraught and mixed-up public" (5). Its status as transgressive film was built into the marketing campaign used to promote it. An end title to the film asked audiences to keep the ending of this "movie which dared to be different" to themselves. Secrecy, endemic to the film's content, became part of the film's marketing campaign as well.

Rhoda is a transgressive subject not just because she is a murderer, but because she is a murderer who is a child. Underneath her flawless exterior she harbors the transgressive desire to murder. Rhoda illustrates Bataille's argument that transgression shows the utmost respect for the law. One aspect of Rhoda that is disturbing is her lack of ordinary flaws. While she commits the ultimate act of transgression in murder, she never violates minor taboos. Miss Fern comments on her perfect curtsey. Christine remarks to Monica Breedlove (Evelyn Varden) that Rhoda never gets her clothes dirty or her shoes scuffed. Rhoda always keeps her room neat. She displays the utmost respect for rules. Even after committing the murders, Rhoda's greatest fear is of being caught. Her murder of LeRoy is predicated on her fear that he has found the shoes used to murder Claude and will turn her in. Even after transgressing the law in the worst possible ways, Rhoda venerates it through her intense fear of being caught.

Further, the film itself venerates the taboo that Rhoda transgresses. Rhoda's death at the end of the film, which differs from the novel and play versions, indicates that Rhoda's monstrous transgression must be punished.[2] As Simmons notes, "Using an act of God to punish Rhoda may well have been bad drama, but it did much to resolve Shurlock's doubts about *The Bad Seed*. God's intervention provided a fitting object lesson for those 'impressionable children'" (5).[3] As William Paul observes, the ending was a secret not just for the audience, but was "kept secret even from the cast members and locked away in a studio vault"

(278). Rhoda's transgression hence does not so much affirm a belief in the legal system, as many detective films do, but it affirms a belief in the divine. This reaffirmation of a belief in a higher power links it firmly with horror films.[4] Yet, the fact that God himself must punish Rhoda's crimes indicates the transgressive nature of a child who kills both other children and adults.

Rhoda's transgressions, just like the film's explanation for them, exist on the cusp between animal and human behavior. Bataille maintains that only humans are capable of transgression because they live in a society built by taboos. Bataille argues that cruelty is a conscious intention "in a mind which has resolved to trespass into a forbidden field of behavior" (*Erotism* 80). It is the human's awareness of this trespass that defines transgression. Shurlock's concern that children might consciously choose to emulate Rhoda's behavior suggests just such an understanding of her transgressions. Yet, *The Bad Seed* is ambivalent about Rhoda's conscious control over her actions. Discussing the animal's killing of another animal, Bataille comments that "the apathy that the gaze of the animal expresses after the combat is the sign of an existence that is essentially on a level with the world in which it moves like water" (*Religion* 25). This apathetic gaze could be used to describe Rhoda's reaction after committing the murders. When Rhoda returns from the picnic and her murder of Claude, she asks her mother for a peanut butter sandwich and seems primarily concerned with having missed her lunch. She tells Christine, "I don't feel any way at all." After setting the excelsior on fire and locking LeRoy in the cellar for his fiery death Rhoda calmly returns to the house and begins playing the piano.[5] On one level, then, the film posits that Rhoda's acts are not truly transgressions, because she is not conscious of them as such. Further, the biological explanation of the bad seed works to remove blame from Rhoda.[6]

Simultaneously, Rhoda does seem aware that she is violating the law. Rhoda pleads with Christine not to tell Miss Fern about the medal. When Christine tells her not to inform anybody else about the murder, Rhoda coolly replies, "Why would I tell and get killed?" The film wants to posit Rhoda as the scandalous, transgressive child, but also wants to pull back from the implications of that by blaming the bad seed that controls her actions and motivations.

While Rhoda's transgressions are those of murder, *The Bad Seed* makes a connection between Rhoda's transgressions and sexual transgression. In the original ad campaign promoting the transgressive nature of the film, a poster displaying Rhoda was replaced by "ads ignoring the child and featuring a woman, clad in a transparent negligee, 'THE BAD SEED IS THE BIG SHOCKER!' headed the ad with a 'Recommended for ADULTS ONLY' warning featured prominently." As Simmons notes, this ad brought larger crowds to the film (10). The novel makes an explicit link between Rhoda's violence and sexual transgression. LeRoy's fascination with Rhoda is given an obvious erotic overtone in the novel. The narrator of the novel describes LeRoy's feelings for Rhoda: "Leroy remained on the steps for a time, smoking his pipe and thinking of the little Penmark girl. He would have been surprised to know that, in a sense, he was in love with the little girl, and that his persecution of her, his nagging concern with everything she did, was part of a perverse and frightened courtship" (54). While the film is much less explicit in connecting LeRoy's tormenting of Rhoda with sexual desire, Christine is shown warning LeRoy not to speak to Rhoda. When Reginald Tasker encounters Rhoda in the film he says that she makes him wish he had married, and comments that "there's a little ray of sunshine . . . She's going to make some man very happy, just that smile." Rhoda's transgressions make her sexually attractive to men. Christine expresses concern over Rhoda's "mature" quality to Miss Fern.

The link between criminal transgression and sexual transgression is established in *The Bad Seed* in several other ways as well. The bad seed, as the ad campaign for the film suggested, encoded both criminal and sexual transgression. Two of Rhoda's three victims are at least potentially sexually transgressive themselves. LeRoy's pedophilia is the most obvious, but the novel implies that Claude is a potential homosexual.[7] The connection between criminal tendencies and transgressive sexuality was a commonplace of cold war society. Benshoff notes that the most visible link between homosexuality and criminality in the 1950s was the direct connection between communism and homosexuality: "homosexuality became directly connected to communism both in the popular press and in the public gestalt from February of 1950, when hearings before the Senate Appropriations Committee revealed that homosexuality had been the reason for recent dismissals of government workers" (130). The film version situates the transgressions of Rhoda within a cold war environment, specifying what, in March's novel, is largely ahistorical criminality.

The film explicitly links the violence of Rhoda's world to cold war society.[8] In the opening scene, as Kenneth Penmark leaves for his secret assignment in Washington DC, Monica tells him to try to stop a war because "I'm not ready to be turned into a piece of chalk just yet." Fear of nuclear war is the first fear expressed in the film. Further, the film alters Kenneth's profession from the businessman he is in the novel to military colonel. As critics have noted, it is Kenneth's absence that seems to make Rhoda's bad behavior break out.[9] Yet, Rhoda's transgressions seem to mirror the transgressions of a cold war military with its ostensible plans for nuclear war and very real radiation experiments on human subjects. The secrets and lies that hide behind Rhoda's perfect exterior seem to characterize her society as a whole. Rhoda's reaction to the attempt to revive Claude's body—"Oh, but I thought it was exciting!"—might be Kenneth's reaction to a nuclear bomb test, one that perhaps utilized military troops in order to test the effects of radiation on human subjects.[10] It is the excelsior from the tea set that Kenneth mails to Rhoda that she sets fire to in order to murder LeRoy. In her attempt to absolve Rhoda of blame for Claude's death Miss Fern describes Rhoda as being "like a soldier" who deserted under fire. Yet, Miss Fern knows the truth, but conceals it. Rhoda's admonition to LeRoy—"You lie all the time!"—might be directed at any of the adult characters in the film, as Miss Fern observes when she tells Christine that all adults have lied. Perhaps this explains why a *deus ex machina* must destroy Rhoda. Because all the characters in the film are transgressors, because there is doubt expressed about the authority structures and their ability to maintain taboos, God must intervene and destroy the threat of Rhoda. Rhoda is the sacrifice because she has revealed the transgression necessary to reinforce the taboos of cold war culture. Rhoda has revealed the transgression that underlies American cold war society and its taboos.

The Fly (1958) more explicitly links transgression to the cold war arms race. The film is structured as a mystery as François Delambre attempts to understand why his sister-in-law Hélène (Patricia Owens) killed her husband André, François' brother. Hélène reveals that she has killed André at his own request after his experiments with a disintegrator/integrator device resulted in his atoms being fused with those of a fly. She killed a "thing," consisting of her husband's body, the fly's head, and one of the fly's arms. Inspector Charas, who has listened to Hélène's story, does not believe her, and attempts to have her committed to an insane asylum. At the last moment Hélène's son, Philippe, discovers the fly containing André's head and arm about to be devoured by a spider. Charas takes pity on the thing and kills it. François tells him that now he is as much a murderer as Hélène is, and Charas releases her.

The most obvious transgression *The Fly* deals with is one that is conventional to science fiction and horror films in general, and especially those produced during the cold war period. In one of the original trailers for the film Vincent Price tells the audience that the film is a shocking story in which "a man actually dared to play God." When André first shows Hélène the disintegrator/integrator he tells her, "Hélène, you're the first to see a miracle." After André's transformation into the monstrosity he types a message to Hélène, in which these words appear: "There are things man should never experiment with." The film explicitly links André's assumption of the god/scientist role with atomic-age fears. In a conversation that takes place in the laboratory Hélène expresses fear of the present, commenting on "the suddenness of our age." After listing many recent discoveries she laments, "Everything's going so fast."[10] George Langelaan's story, on which the film is based, opens by expressing a fear of technological change as François, as narrator, laments that telephones are intrusions that no longer allow men to be the masters in their own homes (343). In affirmation of his fear he receives a call from Hélène telling him that she has just used a hydraulic press to kill André. In the flashback when we are shown the destruction of André, we see Hélène forced to push a button in order to drop the press a second time. Thus, the pressing of a technological button destroys André's life and hides all proof of his transgression. On this level *The Fly* operates routinely within a sf/horror framework of condemning radical scientific experimentation as transgressive while simultaneously lauding that very experimentation. At the end of the film François encourages Phillipe to follow in his father's footsteps and continue "searching for the truth." In *The Return of the Fly* (1959) Phillipe takes up the suggestion by repeating his father's transgression. Thus, within the realm of scientific experimentation, taboo and transgression are mutually reinforcing. The condemnation of new scientific discovery as blasphemous makes it an alluring area of pursuit, especially when the pursuit is financially lucrative, as it was in the cold war Era. When François examines André's laboratory he tells Hélène that he has been allowed in the lab only three times and each time he has visited it meant profit for their business. François further tells Charas that both he and André "have more money that we know what to do with." Thus the transgression implicit in cold war weapons development hinted at in *The Bad Seed* is brought explicitly to the forefront in *The Fly*.

Yet, the discovery of scientific transgression is one that occurs later in the film's narrative. The film frames itself immediately as one of violent erotic transgression as Hélène phones François and tells him, "I killed André. I need your help."[11] Thus the murder of André appears to be one within the framework of the erotic connection between Hélène and André. François tells Charas that "They were completely happy together . . . Hélène was always so gentle . . . It's impossible." Charas' first reaction to the murder is to suspect François because he realizes that François is in love with Hélène. Indeed, Hélène's transgression in the film is an erotic one. Because she loves André so thoroughly she helps him destroy himself and takes on the burden of preserving his secret even to the extent of putting her own life at risk to do so.

For both Hélène and André the secrecy of the scientific experiment is conjoined with the secrecy of their erotic attachment. Bataille argues that "the foundation of eroticism is the sexual act. Now, this act is subject to a prohibition. It's inconceivable! Making love is *prohibited*! Unless you do it in secret. But if we do it in secret the prohibition transfigures what it prohibits and illuminates it with a glow, at once sinister and divine: in a word, it illumines it with a religious glow" (*Tears* 66). In several key scenes in the film André's sharing of his scientific secret with Hélène is framed within eroticism. When André first demonstrates the device to Hélène he uses a wedding present they were given to make the demonstration. Bataille argues that marriage is a paradoxical transgression because just as sacrifice lifts the ban on killing, so does marriage lift the ban on sexual activity (*Erotism* 109). The invoking of André and Hélène's wedding thus indicates that just as marriage is a permitted transgression in a society in which sexuality is taboo, so is radical scientific experimentation a permitted transgression, at least as long as it is successful. Later in the film, the connection between André's and Hélène's erotic feelings for each other and André's experiment is brought out even more clearly. After attending the ballet together André takes Hélène to the laboratory to drink champagne as a prelude to lovemaking. André puts the champagne through the device and attempts to assuage Hélène's fears by saying that the new scientific discoveries are "wonderful facts . . . which brings me back to the champagne." Hélène responds by saying, "It's wonderful being married to you."

André's transformation serves as a strange echo of the intense erotic bond between him and Hélène. Bataille argues that "the final aim of eroticism is fusion, all barriers gone" (*Erotism* 129). André's physical fusion with the fly represents the type of complete erotic union with Hélène he has been seeking. Prior to putting himself through the device he asks Hélène if she would marry him over again. Instead, he finds himself in a perverse marriage with the fly. Bataille argues that the transgressive value of eroticism lies in its attempt to achieve unity with the sacred world, a unity that would result in the obliteration of the personality, an obliteration connected with death. Bataille comments that a love between a man and a woman always "involves the idea of death, murder or suicide. This aura of death is what denotes passion" (*Erotism* 20). The monster that André becomes and Hélène's willingness to destroy this monster at the cost of her own life embodies the couple's transgressive erotic desire for each other as well as André's desire for scientific discovery. In Langelaan's story this point is made even more forcefully as Hélène kills herself by taking cyanide. André's last words scrawled on the blackboard from which he has erased his scientific formulae are "Love You."

The film suggests that the cold war push for scientific discovery carries with it a dangerous transgressive desire. Robert Sasso argues that Bataille's theory forces us to acknowledge that "the rational, in opposing itself to the irrational, would only 'absolutely' constitute itself to the extent that it would paradoxically liberate the latter with some commotion" (44). Edward Teller justified and continued to justify the hydrogen bomb project by arguing that those who opposed nuclear technology opposed progress ("Interview" 3). However, a push for scientific discovery during the cold war that predicated itself on a reasonable pursuit of progress in fact served to unleash irrational desire, such as is manifested in André transformed into a monstrous creature of transgressive desire.

Like *The Bad Seed* and *The Fly*, *Psycho* (1960) uses the horror genre to explore transgression and taboo within the framework of cold war society. *Psycho* focuses first on Marion Crane, a real-estate secretary, who longs to marry her boyfriend, Sam Loomis, but cannot, due to financial constraints. Returning from a rendezvous with Sam at a local motel, Marion steals money from her boss, $40,000 that she is supposed to deposit in the bank, a cash transaction brought to the office by Tom Cassidy, a vulgar client of the real estate agency. Marion then begins driving toward Sam, who lives in Fairvale, California. Overwhelmed by rain she stops at the Bates Motel, where she meets Norman Bates a seemingly nice but lonely young man. Marion resolves to return the money but is brutally stabbed in the shower by Norman's mother. Sam, Marion's sister, Lila, and Arbogast, a private detective, begin looking for Marion. Arbogast traces her to the motel and attempts to speak to Mrs. Bates, but is brutally stabbed by her. Sam and Lila investigate at the motel, and Lila discovers Mrs. Bates in the fruit cellar, revealing that she is a stuffed corpse and that Norman has been dressing as her and committing the murders. A psychiatrist sums up Norman's state of mind, arguing that after murdering his mother and her lover, he began to be possessed by the personality of Mrs. Bates. Now, her personality has taken over.

Psycho represents Hitchcock's most explicit connection to the horror genre and his most blatant attempt to use transgression as both content in a film and as a marketing strategy. Christopher Nickens notes that Hitchcock conceived the idea for making *Psycho* based on the success of low-budget horror films by directors such as William Castle and Roger Corman (qtd. in Leigh 5). While these films had been labeled as "bargain basement Hitchcock," the director decided to take "the opportunity to beat his cheapjack imitators at their own game" (qtd. in Leigh 5). Hitchcock deliberately cast a pall of secrecy over the filming of *Psycho*. A commentator in the *New York Times* in December 1959 noted the secrecy Hitchcock was maintaining around his new film project: "Moreover, and again violating standard studio policy, no story synopsis will be released. The only previous example of this synopsis veto was in the case of *The Ten Commandments* when rumor had it that the late Cecil B. DeMille refused to sanction a story synopsis—lest it give away the plot" (Merrick n.p.). Janet Leigh discusses the secrecy and sense of transgression surrounding the project. Commenting on a nude model who was hired as a stand-in for the role of Marion, Leigh comments "I think Hitch deliberately hired the model partly to plant the seed in people's minds that this picture had nudity. He had started to manipulate the audiences before the film was even in a theatre. He teased the pros, the nonpros, the sophisticated, and the naïve" (76). Like *The Bad Seed*, *Psycho* demanded that the viewer, after having seen the film, should not give away the shocking ending.

Early negative critical response to the film was created partly by Hitchcock's refusal to allow the press to attend advance screenings, though a large part of the adverse criticism was produced by the transgressive nature of its subject matter. An article by Bosley Crowther in the *New York Times* was titled "An Answer to Those Filmgoers Who Think 'Psycho' Should be Banned." In a letter written to the *New York Times*, a Mrs. Frank Nowve lambasted *Psycho* because "It is deliberately calculated to stimulate the jaded appetites of the middle-aged and arouse the worst latent instincts of teen-agers" ("Letters"). Like reactions to *The Bad Seed*, some reactions to *Psycho* suggested that the transgression depicted on the screen might, in fact, be contagious. What transgression frightened some of the early viewers of *Psycho*?

The first transgression *Psycho* presents us with is erotic transgression. Several of the early posters advertising the film depict Marion in her underwear forefront and Norman in the background, hence highlighting the erotic as the means of enticing viewers. The opening sequence depicting Sam and Marion's erotic encounter takes us into a world not so much of sexual transgression but of erotic transgression. Marion's intense love for Sam makes this a transgressive act as it will serve as the catalyst for her robbery of the money. Premarital sexuality may have been officially a taboo in the late 1950s, but in practice, it had been common among middle-class Americans at least since the 1940s. Sex and marriage manuals of the 1950s indicate that the most striking change in sexual behavior among postwar women was the high incidence of premarital intercourse between women and their fiancés. Ernest M. Burgess and Paul Wallin in *Engagement and Marriage* (1953) note that "the great majority of the women who had premarital relations had them only with the men they subsequently married" (330). Yet, as Burgess and Wallin note, premarital intercourse posed a dilemma for women because while there existed pressure to engage in it, female virginity before marriage still held great currency in the 1950s. Burgess and Wallin relate female uncertainty about sexuality with what most 1950s commentators see as the largest sexual problem of the time—female frigidity. They conclude that the 1950s woman "is conditioned to be sexually frigid" (696-97). Albert Ellis calls female frigidity *The American Sexual Tragedy* in his 1954 book. Ellis comments that women "become emotionally upset when they do and when they do not engage in some form of premarital sexual activity. They frequently turn out to be orgasmically frigid . . . on the whole, they seem to derive about one-tenth of the sexual satisfaction and fulfillment of which they are potentially capable when they and their mates are fully sexually released and mature" (72). Marion's love for Sam has caused her to sacrifice her virginity to him and her frustration stems from the fact that he postpones marriage. In the opening sequence Marion's transgressive erotic desire for Sam sets her up as a sacrificial figure as she says to him, "I pay, too. They also pay who meet in hotel rooms." Thus while Sam pays financially through his bondage to his father's debts, Marion pays emotionally by having to meet Sam in secret. In his famous interviews with François Truffaut, Hitchcock commented on the opening sequence in the following manner: "In the opening of *Psycho* I wanted to say that we were in Phoenix, and we even spelled out the day and time, but I only did that to lead up to a very important fact: that it was two-forty-three in the afternoon and this is the only time the poor girl has to go to bed with her lover. It suggests that she's spent her whole lunch hour with him" (266).

The sympathy that the film creates for the character of Marion is predicated on her transgressive desire, a desire that exceeds that of those around her. The screenwriter of *Psycho*, Joseph Stefano, commenting on the film stated:

I think what attracts me is the human condition that ultimately, basically, we are all alone. And that the only thing that makes fire is when somebody else who is alone collides with us in an emotional way, and then we have love. So my feeling was this story in regard to Marion was all about her love; everything she did, even to being killed, was about her love. And that made her a love character. (qtd. in Leigh 60)

Janet Leigh writes that she was drawn to the part because "I really cared about Marion Crane" (37). Many critics have expressed similar feelings for her character.[12] In creating a situation in which the viewer is encouraged to intensely identify with a character who is motivated by erotic transgression, a transgression that causes her to break the law and die a tragic, random death, *Psycho* illustrates to us the power of what Bataille sees as the sacred.[14] Bataille argues that "Only the extremism of desire and death enables one to attain the truth" (*Impossible* 9). Marion transgresses the taboo on excessive erotic desire and this causes her to violate the taboo on stealing, but the money is not important, acquisition is not at the base of Marion's motives; expenditure is. Bataille argues that eroticism illustrates that what we desire uses us up and often endangers our lives (*Accursed* II, 104). As Marion plots to steal the money she complains of a headache. Cassidy tells her that she needs a weekend in Las Vegas. Marion replies, "I'm going to spend this weekend in bed," expressing the desire to be in bed with Sam that motivates the theft. After returning home to pack, Marion places the money on the bed, again indicating its status as signifier of her erotic desire for Sam.

The film juxtaposes her reckless desire with Sam's cautious desire for her. Sam represents a character who understands limited transgression, but not the full erotic transgression Marion enacts. Bataille argues that true lovers work to negate society that is at odds with their desires (*Accursed* II, 159). While this statement would easily apply to Marion's attempt to negate the social in favor of her desire, Sam seems to stand for the very taboo she violates.[15] Leigh notes that in early conversations with Stefano "he mentioned that he had always felt that Marion loved Sam more than Sam loved her" (55). Leigh replied to him that "As it stood, Sam had no problem and no commitment" (56). In Robert Bloch's novel, on which the film is based, Sam's lack of emotional involvement with Marion is made even clearer as following Mary's (Marion's name in the novel) disappearance Sam questions his desire for her: "Sometimes he wondered if they hadn't made a mistake when they planned ahead. After all, what did they really know about each other?" (84). While Sam seems to enjoy the illicitness of his desire for Marion, his feelings are not truly transgressive, because he does not seek to reaffirm the taboo through desire. Marion's intense desire to marry Sam indicates how her transgressive acts venerate the taboo they appear to violate.

Marion's flight to Sam illustrates how in the logic of the film taboos reinforce transgression. Marion encounters a series of authority figures—Lowery, the policeman, California Charlie—who suspect her but let her continue on her flight. Even though Marion practically advertises her guilt through her reckless actions, they allow her to go. When she asks the policeman "Have I broken any laws?" he replies that she has not. The figures of authority seem to fuel her flight instead of causing her to stop. Only in her imagination is Marion punished for her transgressions, most chillingly when she imagines Cassidy saying he will take the money out of "her fine, soft flesh," a premonition of the sacrificial victim she will become.[15] When Marion does become a sacrifice, it is when she encounters the monstrous double of her own erotic desire.

Critics have noted the doubling between Marion and Norman that the film presents.[16] Raymond Bellour argues that initially upon viewing the film it appears that "the psychiatrist's commentary on Norman Bates has little to do with the love scene between Marion and Sam in the Phoenix hotel" (105). Bellour argues that the film is split, as our sympathies shift from the subject of neurosis (Marion) to the subject of psychosis (Norman). Following Bellour, I argue that Marion's transgressive desire for erotic fusion with Sam in marriage is taken to psychotic lengths in Norman's transgressive desire for erotic fusion with his mother. Thus Marion is not punished for her transgressive desire by an authority figure but, rather, is sacrificed by yet another transgressor in the form of Norman. Norman attains his fusion with Mrs. Bates only after her death; Marion also hideously achieves her desired fusion with Sam after death. William Rothman notes that "*Psycho's* great irony has Sam finally penning a letter to Marion in which he admits she was right, as her dead body, crammed in the trunk of the car, lies at the bottom of the swamp" (256). Further, as Lesley Brill notes, "Later, Lila will play out with Sam the sort of domestic scenes that Marion hoped to buy with Cassidy's money and for which she paid with her life" (228). Bloch's novel compounds his terrible irony by having Sam passionately kiss Lila when she arrives at his store because he has mistaken her for Marion (85).

Yet, the character who most closely mirrors Marion's transgression is one who also pays for her erotic desire with death as well, the other sacrificed woman in the film—Mrs. Bates. If one believes the psychiatrist's comments about Mrs. Bates, she was "a clinging, demanding woman" who warped Norman into the psycho we see in the film. Yet, critics have frequently disputed the psychiatrist's characterization of Mrs. Bates.[17] Bloch's novel lays the groundwork for such a reading. It lays the blame most often on Norman himself: "There had been other widows, other only sons, and not all of them became enmeshed in this sort of relationship. It was really his fault as much as hers. Because he didn't have any gumption" (14). Norman reveals to Mary that the desire between them is more than likely one-sided: "I tell myself that she'd be lost without me, now—maybe the real truth is that I'd be even more lost without *her*" (42). Norman tells Mary that he stopped Mrs. Bates from remarrying: "You don't have to tell me about jealousy, possessiveness— I was worse than she could ever be" (44). Thus, Mother of the film may well be only Norman's creation of a mother who needs him. As Rothman argues, we cannot dismiss the sheriff's original story "that Norman's mother killed her lover when she found out that he was married, then poisoned herself, with Norman discovering both bodies in bed" (333). If we accept this explanation Mrs. Bates emerges as a woman very like Marion Crane, a woman who followed her erotic desire to the point of death itself.

The Bates' house suggests a woman enmeshed in the erotic. The physical sign of Mrs. Bates apart from her corpse is the heavy indentation in her bed. The sign she has left behind is the sign of her intense and transgressive desire for a married man. As Tom Bauso has argued, the figure of Cupid that appears in the Bates' house suggests that Mrs. Bates was not puritanical but was "a sexually mature woman with more than a passing interest in the world of Eros" (6). Like Marion's, perhaps Mrs. Bates' erotic transgression also made her an object of sacrifice, whether Norman killed her or she killed herself. If Norman killed her, she stands, like Marion as the victim of sacrifice, but a sacrifice with no social purpose. Thus their transgressions ultimately do not serve to reinforce taboo. The psychotic transgression of Norman's desire also fulfills no such purpose.

Psycho, then, in a much less obvious way than *The Bad Seed* or *The Fly,* highlights the operations of taboo and transgression in the cold war. While mention of cold war concerns are never explicitly made, critics have read the film as implicitly dealing with anxieties endemic to the postwar political and social scene.[18] Within the framework of Bataille's theories of taboo and transgression, *Psycho* suggests disturbing aspects of cold war society. While Bataille argued that erotic transgression was one means of channeling the sacred into a form that would avoid the catastrophe of war, Norman's psychotic eroticism suggests a form of transgression very similar to war. Norman kills random, innocent victims, and does so blindly. George Toles argues that Norman has learned to "see and do the things that are forbidden to him without actually seeing anything. That is to say, the face of his presence and involvement in acts that are literally unthinkable for him is 'dropped from the frame.' As the mother blindly wields the knife, Norman's eyes are somewhere else, trying to stay focused on what is decent" (641). Norman's acts suggest a blind transgression. While Bataille's transgressors are aware of the taboos they break, and, because of this awareness, reaffirm the taboo and the ongoing desire to violate the taboo in a system that works to make society cohesive, Norman transgresses without consciously knowing that he is doing so. It his unknowingness that makes him stand as the most frightening of cold war transgressors. Rhoda kills for acquisition of objects or to protect her secret. Hélène is fully aware of the implications of pushing the red button that will result in the death of the monstrous André. Norman embodies the fear of one who pushes the button blindly, bringing about random destruction of innocent victims.

While Norman represents the Other living within the apparently normal cold war man, other fifties horror films, from both the United States and Britain, imagined an external Other that represented the horror of the foreign, and, specifically, Communist, threat.

The next section of the book looks at British and American horror films in juxtaposition. British films revitalized the horror genre in the 1950s through Hammer Studios. *The BFI Companion to Horror* states that Hammer "led the world market in horror, inspired many imitations and today retains a significant hold on the affections of genre aficionados" (144). Examining several British and American films' representations of evil Others sheds light on eroticism and taboo in both cultures.

Part II

Evil Others

VAMPIRES IN COLD WAR FILM

Within the world of horror, the postwar vampire found himself eclipsed by a new kind of impersonal monster, one that was the product of the atomic bomb and the horrors of total war. The evil Others of cold-war horror found expression in both American and British horror films. In both the fiction and film of the 1950s the vampire is generally marginalized or made to conform to fantasies of anti-communism and post-nuclear-war holocaust. Yet, by the end of the decade, British horror films reasserted the mythic eroticism of Dracula in Hammer Films' 1958 picture *The Horror of Dracula*. In this chapter, I explore the British horror genre's ability to reinvigorate the cold war vampire with mythic sexuality, an ability that contrasts with American horror's draining of the vampire by casting him as the monster of McCarthyist and nuclear-war fantasies.

One power of the vampire myth lies in its ability to transmutate from age to age and culture to culture by tapping into fears and desires regarding death and sexuality. As Joan Gordon and Veronica Hollinger argue vis-à-vis the continuing power of the vampire myth, "An ambiguously coded figure, a source of both erotic anxiety and corrupt desire, the literary vampire is one of the most powerful archetypes bequeathed to us from the imagination of the nineteenth century" (1). While Gordon and Hollinger maintain that the vampire myth survives because "we do indeed see many diverse reflections—of ourselves—as the vampire stands before us cloaked in metaphor" (3), the vampire's connection to seemingly ashistorical forces such as sexuality and death also explain its allure.

Nostalgia for the vampire and the world he or she embodies is frequently predicated on a perception that the vampire can link us to something beyond the historical. Thus, the vampire assumed a problematic status in an age bound up in contemporary politics and their perceived ability through nuclear war to end life as we know it. Nina Auerbach speculates that the "rhetoric of Armageddon" attached to the postwar period created an age "sparse in monsters" (117). While monsters of a different type populated 1950s sf/horror fiction and film, the dark seduction of the vampire seemed unable to function as an appropriate metaphor for the anxieties of the atomic age. As the *BFI Companion to Horror* notes, the typical fifties vampire works were a hybrid of sf and horror, with Richard Matheson's *I Am Legend* (1954) illustrative of the trend (322).[1]

The vampire as metaphor yokes together sexuality and death, and points to an erotic desire that seems to be outside history. For Bataille, eroticism's allure stems from such a desire to escape the confines of historical time and capture experience that is ahistorical. For Bataille, the lover's desire is a desire for annihilation, a yearning to destroy the individual existence and merge with something that is continuous. Eroticism longs for death as a figure for this desire for continuity. In Bataille's imagination, the statue-like woman possessed by erotic desire is a metaphor for desire itself that strives to go beyond individuality, that seeks a continuity masquerading as death.

For Bataille, as for vampire mythology, the scene of erotic power is located in the seduction of a beautiful woman. Bataille paints a scene of erotic aestheticism in the following manner, one that recalls the vampire's victim: "Imagine the incomparable beauty of a woman who happens to be dead. She's not a living being, there's nothing to be understood about her. No one's in the bedroom. God's not. The room's empty" (*Guilty* 80). Ultimately, the power of the erotic in Bataille is imagined in the aesthetically pleasing, possessed, and sometimes dead woman: she represents the possibility of escaping the immediacy of history. When lovers unite in Bataille's world they give up the social for the universal (*Visions* 252).

It is precisely this recapturing of the erotic as antidote to cold war historical specificity that Hammer Films offered its audience in *The Horror of Dracula*. The film is an adaptation of Bram Stoker's novel *Dracula* that embodies significant plot changes. Jonathan Harker seeks Dracula out at the behest of Dr. Van Helsing, but is seduced by Dracula's bride, resulting in his transformation into a vampire. Van Helsing destroys Jonathan, then returns home to find Lucy Holmwood, Jonathan's fiancée, already the victim of Dracula. After Lucy's destruction at the hands of Van Helsing and Arthur Holmwood, Lucy's brother, Dracula begins preying on Mina Holmwood, Lucy's sister-in-law. Holmwood and Van Helsing save Mina from final transformation when they discover Dracula's coffin in the Holmwood wine cellar. Van Helsing exposes Dracula to rays of sunlight, and the vampire disintegrates.

In the documentary *Flesh and Blood: The Hammer Heritage of Horror*, the filmmakers locate Hammer Studio's success in the 1950s in its ability to blend eroticism with a return to the conventions of classic horror films. While American 1950s horror films that didn't combine with sf elements had fallen into decline due to tongue-in-cheek versions of horror such as *Abbott and Costello Meet Dr. Jekyll and Mr. Hyde*

(1953) and *Abbott and Costello Meet the Mummy* (1955), Hammer recuperated the seriousness of horror by eschewing the camp approach. In *Flesh and Blood*, Peter Cushing, who played Van Helsing in the Hammer Dracula films, comments that the films were never meant to be tongue-in-cheek. The serious tone of the Hammer films allowed a recuperation of the mythic power of the vampire to occur. As *The BFI Companion to Horror* notes, "Hammer revived the fortunes of the traditional vampire with *Dracula*" (322).

In 1958, when Universal allowed Hammer Studios to remake the Universal classic *Dracula,* the studio sought to infuse Dracula with sex appeal. Director Terence Fisher commented that "Dracula is a tremendously sensual creature . . . When he comes down those stairs, you see this totally attractive man, not a twisted grotesque" (qtd. in Flynn 86). Christopher Lee, who played Dracula in the film, states that he played Dracula as a "malevolent hero" (*Flesh and Blood*). One of the posters for *The Horror of Dracula* described Dracula as a "terrifying lover who died, yet lived." As *Flesh and Blood* relates, early viewers were struck by the film's sexual explicitness. Director Joe Dante recalls being impressed by the "parade of buxom British starlets" (*Flesh and Blood*). Nina Auerbach, recalling her own youthful experience of the film, reflects on the allure of Christopher Lee, describing him as "brisk and entrepreneurial, more up to date than the little men who scurry around to protect their strapping, sexy women" (119). Importantly, as *Flesh and Blood* makes clear, the eroticism of *The Horror of Dracula* takes place not within any historically specific world, but in the "insular fantasy world" created by Hammer Films.[2]

Yet, the film's relocation of the vampire to mythical time was not an easy one. Wartime propaganda films had marked the vampire as fascist villain. Rick Worland discusses the use of Bela Lugosi in wartime propaganda films, such as *Black Dragons* (1942). This film "associates the supernatural threat of Dracula with a popularized caricature of fascist ideology" (49). Though, as Worland argues, the fit between horror films and propaganda films was never a smooth one, the attempt to make the ancient threat of the vampire into a historically specific one troubled the horror genre after the war. Traces of the association between Nazi and vampire exist in *The Horror of Dracula*. The revised German/Swiss setting for the film, which removes the London/Transylvania split of the novel, encodes anxiety related to the possible resurgence of a Nazi threat. The sheer exuberance of the film, however, with its celebration of Dracula's power seems not so much ideological as mythical, as an attempt to escape World War II and cold war boundaries by celebrating the sexual.[3]

The opening sequence of the film, with blood spattering over Dracula's name embossed on his coffin, takes us into a brightly colored world of sexuality and death. Auerbach argues that the Hammer series relied on the formulaic plots of vampire myth, yet changed the focus of the vampire from the hypnotic eyes of Universal's vampires to the sensuous mouth. She states that because the Hammer Studio's vampires were "the first movie vampires to be associated with mouths rather than mesmeric powers, they turned vampirism into an immediate bodily experience rather than an esoteric endowment" (129).[4] The eroticism of Lucy's open sexual invitation to Dracula as she opens the door and awaits Dracula's arrival in bed, even arranging the pillow for him as one would for a lover, highlights the cruel eroticism that lies at the heart of the film.[5] Like Bataille's lovers, Lucy and Mina thrive on a sexuality that obliterates them, that takes them beyond the immediate world into a connection with the continuous. In the secular, erotic world of *The Horror of Dracula*, Van Helsing does not worry about the victims' souls, as does the Van Helsing of Stoker's novel, but makes an analogy between the desire of the victims and drug addiction.

The erotic revitalized vampire is also at the center of Hammer Studio's *The Brides of Dracula* (1960). This film focuses on Baroness Meinster, a German woman who protects and feeds her vampire son by bringing him young women to feed upon. When she picks up Marianne, a young woman traveling to a girl's academy to take up a teaching position, her world changes. Marianne falls in love with the son, Baron Meinster, and releases him. The Baron bites his mother and transforms her into a vampire. He then immediately attacks a village girl. The girl escapes in vampire form. Meanwhile, Dr. Van Helsing arrives in town to help the local priest with the mysterious occurrences. He begins to investigate and soon concludes that the Baron is a vampire. The Baron visits Marianne at the girls' academy and becomes engaged to her. He then kills and transforms Gina, one of Marianne's colleagues. Van Helsing tracks the Baron and his brides to an old mill where he defeats the Baron with holy water and saves Marianne from transformation.

As in *The Horror of Dracula*, the emphasis in *The Brides of Dracula* is upon the erotic power of the vampire and his ability to sexually awaken his victims. Because she is a woman traveling alone Marianne becomes an object of suspicion in the village she stops at. The villagers do not warn her of the danger of the Castle Meinster, but, rather, becomes accomplices when they allow the Baroness to take her away to the castle as a victim for her son. The narrator at the opening of the film describes the followers of Dracula as desiring to "corrupt the world," and it is the sexual corruption of Marianne and the Baron's other victims that is emphasized in the film.

When Marianne first encounters the Baron she is struck by his good looks. She is both sexually attracted to him and sympathetic to his plight. He is manacled to the floor, and Marianne believes he is an innocent victim of his mother's madness. The Baron tells Marianne, "you're very beautiful," then entreats her to steal the key to the manacle, if she dares. Marianne interprets the statement as a sexual challenge and tells the Baron, "I dare." Thus, the Baron and his sexual allure is present to corrupt the virginal girls who become his brides—the village girl, Gina, and potentially Marianne.

Yet, as in *The Horror of Dracula*, there is the indication that the virginal girls are longing for sexual corruption and thereby invite the threat. Marianne, through her desire for the Baron, releases him, allowing him to roam free. When the headmaster at the girls' academy, Herr Lang, finds Marianne alone with the Baron, he accuses her of being a "shameless little hussy." Gina envies Marianne's engagement and says, "I wish it had been me." Immediately after making this statement, a bat flies in her window, and the Baron appears before her. After emerging from the coffin as undead, Gina tells Marianne that "we can both love him, my darling," suggesting a ménage à trois between Marianne, Gina, and the Baron. While we do not see the transformation of the village girl, in her transformed state she is a willing follower of the Baron.

As in *The Horror of Dracula*, Van Helsing's fight against the vampire in *The Brides of Dracula* seems to be secular one. While a priest asks for his help and Van Helsing uses crucifixes and holy water in his battle against the Baron, his central concern in the film seems to be a desire to protect Marianne from the Baron, perhaps because he desires her himself. Thus, Van Helsing tells the priest that it is the "vampire's kiss" that causes the transformations. Van Helsing rescues Marianne first, when she is sleeping in the woods after fleeing the Castle Meinster in shock. Van Helsing is very drawn to her and gets her to tell him the story of what has happened in the Castle. Then, he commands that she forget everything. When he learns of her engagement to the Baron, he is horrified, but does not tell her the truth, that the Baron is a vampire. When the Baron and Van Helsing have their showdown at the mill, the Baron taunts Van Helsing by telling him that he will transform Marianne right in front of his eyes. The last image that we see in the film is one of Van Helsing and Marianne embracing as they watch the mill burn. With the implied sexual attraction between Van Helsing and Marianne, the film suggests that hatred of the vampire's eroticism may amount to nothing more than sexual jealousy on the part of the vampire hunter.

What *The Horror of Dracula* and *The Brides of Dracula* did for the postwar vampire was remove him to a mythical world of eroticism and death, far from the black-and-white shadows of an anti-communist and apocalypse-frightened world. As Auerbach argues, young Americans turned to Hammer films because they "led Americans on a mythic return to their glamorous British origin" (126). Meanwhile, back in the United States, vampires were suffocating under the weight of atomic age fear.

Vampire as diseased human, vampire as victim of nuclear war—these scenarios cancel out the eroticism possessed by the nineteenth-century and early twentieth-century vampires. In contrast to the complicated eroticism of vampires in films such as *Dracula's Daughter* (1936) and *Son of Dracula* (1943), the disease metaphor used by American films relates the vampire to post-nuclear-war fallout; it also connects the vampire to McCarthyist concerns over communism as a disease infecting postwar America. In testimony given before HUAC (House Un-American Activities Committee), J. Edgar Hoover utilized a disease metaphor to discuss the communist threat. This metaphor became part of cold war rhetoric. Hoover stated that

Victory will be assured once communists are identified and exposed, because the public will take the first step of quarantining them so they can do no harm. Communism, in reality, is not a political party. It is a way of life—an evil and malignant way of life. It reveals a condition akin to disease that spreads like an epidemic and like an epidemic a quarantine is necessary to keep it from infecting the Nation. (119-20)

The use of the vampire to illustrate disease in cold war American horror films is found in two distinct types of vampire films, those explicitly invoking the traditional tale of the vampire and those that represent a hybrid of science fiction and horror and feature a vampire-like monster.

Amidst a dearth of traditional vampire films, Universal Studios released *Curse of the Undead* in 1959. The film focuses on Drake Robey, the pseudonym of Draco Robles, a Spanish land-grant rancher who kills himself after committing fratricide. After being transformed into a vampire, he returns to reclaim his ranch, which now belongs to the Carter family. Robey kills young girls in the town. He also kills the Carter family's father, and, by fanning a water dispute between the Carter family and a greedy rancher named Buffer, causes the Carter son to be killed. Robey insinuates himself into the good grace of Delores Carter, who is set on getting revenge on Buffer, whom she blames for her father's and brother's deaths. Her boyfriend, preacher Dan Young, unearths Robey's father's diary, thus discovering Robey's true identity as vampire. Young then kills Robey in a gunfight.

The film is a strange hybrid of western and horror film that casts the vampire as McCarthyist disease and does so in a cheerless tone. The opening sequence shows us an empty black-and-white western town, a stark contrast to the colorful, vibrant opening setting of *The Horror of Dracula*. We are immediately placed in a world of illness as a bedside scene shows us a young woman suffering from a mysterious "epidemic affecting only young girls." Vampirism and disease is the first link the film makes. Amidst a dispute over water between two ranches, the vampire moves into town and kills young women and the town doctor without being noticed.

The film casts Drake Robey, the gunfighter vampire, as an unseen malignant influence, like the supposed disease of communism Hoover spoke of. Behind the scenes, Robey effects a breakdown of law and order, inflaming the Carter family against Buffer, and thus causing death as frequently by gunfighting as by blood-sucking. The film works in several ways to link the vampire with a subversive political force. On one level, Robey is opposed to the preacher, Dan Young, who represents religious belief and its ability to battle subversion. Cold war rhetoric frequently distinguished the United States from the Soviet Union on the basis of religious faith. Hoover spoke of the communist threat being "alien to the religion of Christ and Judaism" (119). The 1950s witnessed a religious revival in the United States that stemmed largely from anticommunist sentiment. The immense popularity of evangelists like Billy Graham attested to the United States' need to assert its faith as a means of distinguishing its ideology from that of the Soviet Union.[6]

In *Curse of the Undead,* after the deaths of her father and brother, Delores Carter turns away from Dan Young, embracing vigilantism instead. Young equates vigilantism with devil worship, but Delores defies him, inviting the vampire Robey into her home. Delores' rejection of Young's faith makes her prey to the subversive force of Robey. While Robey can move about in the daylight, drink, and smoke—unconventional behavior for a vampire—he is vulnerable to the cross. Young's cross pin, supposedly carved from a thorn present at the site of the crucifixion, frightens Robey when he first sees it and eventually becomes the means of Robey's death as Young fires a bullet with the cross welded to it into the vampire's heart. As godless subversive force, Robey is vulnerable to American religious belief.

Curse of the Undead absents the erotic lure of vampirism. Although Robey feels love for Delores, her mind is set on revenge. Robey insinuates himself into Delores' ranch house by comparing himself to a soldier. When he visits her bedside to feed on her, none of the erotic invitation of

The Horror of Dracula is present. Delores remains asleep while Robey feeds: she is not an active participant in the act as Lucy is in the Hammer film. During their subsequent meetings, while Drake professes love for Delores, she always remains unconscious. Thus, the scenes are not charged with eroticism, as her motives are only for revenge, and Drake's motives remain obscured. Even though Robey is given a tragic, romantic history, the viewer remains distanced from a cold, unerotic vampire posing as a gunfighter in the old west.

Even a more conventional American vampire film from the same time period casts the vampire as unsympathetic invader. *The Return of Dracula* (1958) purports to revive the alluring count, but instead transforms him into a repulsive, foreign threat to the American way of life. United Artists' B-film focuses on Dracula assuming the identity of an Eastern European immigrant named Bellac Gordal. As Bellac, Dracula travels to Carleton, California, where he murders a young blind woman, and transforms her into a vampire, murders an immigration officer, and attempts to murder and transform another young woman, Rachel Mayberry, whose relative he is posing as. Dracula is inadvertently killed when Rachel and her boyfriend, Tim, cause him to fall into a pit in an abandoned mine and impale himself on a wooden stake.

The Return of Dracula is laced with xenophobia typical of the cold war. The narration that opens the film describes Dracula as "spreading his evil dominion ever wider," thus implicitly linking his vampiric threat with the threat of the spread of communism.[7] Even the real Bellac, who leaves for America to seek freedom—one of his relatives tells him, "you will like America, Bellac, you are lucky to be free"—inadvertently brings disaster to the United States since Dracula is able to assume Bellac's identity and insinuate himself into a typical American home.

Once the film moves its setting to California, its action highlights Dracula's opposition to the American way of life. On the night of his arrival, Dracula refuses to eat dinner with the Mayberry family and their guest, the local preacher, telling Rachel that she must understand his strange behavior. Dracula continually questions why he must conform to American standards. The film emphasizes his status as foreign threat by having his nemesis be not the local preacher, but an immigration officer, Bryant, who asks for his alien-registration papers. When Dracula transforms himself into a vicious dog, he subsequently kills Bryant.

The film goes to lengths to make Dracula repulsive, cold, and unerotic. His first victim is the Mayberry family's pet cat, Nugget, which he finds in an abandoned mine and kills, causing Mickey, Rachel's younger brother, intense emotional pain. His first human victim is Jenny

Blake, a young blind woman Rachel cares for. Dracula visits Jenny and tells her he can free her soul and "take her into the light." She succumbs to him and is transformed into a vampire. In contrast to *The Horror of Dracula,* in which the female victims' complicity in the act of erotic transformation is all-important, Jenny is a complete victim, blind, frightened, and ill. Dracula then sets his sights on Rachel, attempting to force her to reject both her boyfriend and her faith. He tells her not to wear the cross Jenny has given her for protection, because it doesn't "become her." Yet, even in his attempted transformation of Rachel, there is no erotic element. Dracula is a foreign bully who threatens Rachel and Tim with the rhetoric of Armageddon: "We three are the only ones to survive this dying world."

As much as the film vilifies the foreign threat of the Eastern European vampire reimagined as communist spy, it is also firmly rooted in cold war rhetoric because it points to the lack of vigilance on the homefront. Weaknesses in the Mayberry family are factors that allow Dracula to gain dominion. The absence of a father in the house causes Rachel's mother, Cora, to invite Bellac to live with them in California. Most of the blame, however, is placed on Rachel herself. She worships what she sees as refinement in the Eastern European. She taunts her boyfriend for being uncouth in comparison with Bellac. She inadvertently offers Jenny up as a victim to Dracula by asking him to visit her and even leaving the window in her room open so Dracula can enter. Rachel's dangerous attraction to the foreign is also seen in her idealization of Greek society. She wears an ancient Grecian costume to the Halloween party from which Dracula abducts her. Dracula offers Rachel the Old World, stating, "I bring you the dark of centuries past and centuries to come." Rachel learns how dangerous the allure of the corrupt European is; she then appreciates Tim and his embodiment of American youthfulness. The film condemns American fascination with the corrupt ways of Europe. Rachel's inability to recognize the superiority of American culture has almost led to her death and transformation into the undead. American cold war horror's portrayal of the vampire as a repulsive figure is also evident in sf/horror hybrids of the period.

First Man into Space (1959) tells the story of Dan Prescott, a Navy pilot who becomes the first man to fly a jet into space. As the result of passing through a meteorite shower his body becomes encrusted with a protective coating. When he crashes on earth, he is transformed into a monster that must feed on human blood in order to be able to breathe. His brother, Commander Chuck Prescott, solves the mystery of the deaths of cattle and people by tracing the crimes back to Dan. With the help of Doctor Paul von Essen, Chuck attempts to cure Dan by placing him in a high-altitude containment device. Dan regains his humanity and apologizes for what he has done. Then, he dies.

Like *The Horror of Dracula* and *The Brides of Dracula*, *First Man into Space* links transformation into the vampire with sexual transgression. Early on, the film portrays Dan as a reckless man who values pleasure over duty. When he crashes Y-12, the plane he pilots prior to the one that goes into space, Dan leaves the wreckage behind for his brother, Chuck, to deal with. Instead of going back to the base and making a report, he goes to visit his girlfriend, Tia Francesca. When Chuck discovers him there, he upbraids Tia, telling her, "He has no business playing house with you!" Later in the film, after Dan crashes Y-13, Captain Ben Richards of the New Mexico State Police describes the descent of the plane in the following manner: "it came down like a dame in a feather bed." When Dan transforms into a vampire-like creature, his first victim is a beautiful young nurse who works at a blood bank in Albuquerque. Another victim is an attractive young woman whom he kills. He then steals her car, leaving her blood-drained body to be discovered when the police pull him over. Even Dan's murder of a truck driver is intertwined with sexual implications. We see a husband and wife necking as the man prepares to go on a business trip. The man cannot resist kissing his wife again. At that point, Dan appears. The man yells at his wife to not let his side of the bed get cold, to which she replies, "Don't worry, I won't let it get cold." The man gets into the truck and Dan slashes his throat. While sexuality is linked with both the vampire and the victims, *First Man Into Space*, like *Curse of the Undead* and *The Return of Dracula*, makes the vampire not an erotic creature, but a repulsive one.

The vampire Dan first appears as a shadow on the wall outside the blood bank he is about to rob: while the film utilizes the classic image of the shadow of the vampire, arms spread, Dan is repulsive, making animal-like noises and limping. He is more like a Quasimodo than a Dracula. While Dan has the super-human strength and lust for blood typical of the vampire, he is an obvious, hideous-looking monster that resembles a giant rock rather than a seductive charmer. Ben Richards describes Dan as "a great big lumbering deformed monster." The sympathy the film elicits for Dan as vampire is based on the use of a disease metaphor. Whereas *Curse of the Undead* and *The Return of Dracula* use disease metaphors to reference the disease of communism, *First Man into Space* frames the disease of vampirism in a sf context by linking it to scientific discovery and space exploration.

Chuck's investigation of the murders leads him to conclude that Dan is not an evil killer, but one who is sick, one who "kills but only because for some reason or another it needs blood." Dan's disease is representative of the disease of technological advancement that moves too rapidly. Lewis Mumford, for example, perceived 1950s America as a society mentally diseased by rapid technological development: "And the fatal symptoms of their [government's and military's] madness is this: they have been carrying through a series of acts which will lead eventually to the destruction of mankind" ("Gentlemen" 5). *First Man in Space* presents similar conclusions. Dan's recklessness allows him to go into space, but the price he and others must pay is a transformation into a diseased vampire. Chuck tells Tia that this horror has happened to Dan because "We're caught in a new world." Thus, the erotic allure of the vampire is ultimately missing in *First Man in Space*. By associating vampirism with physical monstrosity and disease, the film makes the vampire unappealing.

It! The Terror From Beyond Space (1958) is another sf-horror film that presents the vampire figure as repulsive and alien. This film concerns a mission to Mars during which all crew members but one, Col. Edward Carruthers, have died. Carruthers has been accused of murdering his own crew, and another ship is sent to take him back to Washington for a court martial. After take-off, members of the crew begin mysteriously to disappear. A creature, the one responsible for the deaths of the other crew members, is on the ship. After trying to kill the creature in various ways, the crew, led by Carruthers, eventually kills it by depriving it of oxygen.

The creature possesses several vampire-like characteristics. The first time we see it, it appears in shadow on the wall, playing on the classic *Nosferatu* image also used in *First Man in Space*. The creature displays superhuman strength. A current of electricity that could kill thirty men fails to kill it; exposure to radiation that could kill a hundred men likewise doesn't faze it. It is able to break through metal doors. Bullets do not harm it. Further, it preys on its victims in order to drain all bodily fluids from them. The creature's scratch produces a leukemia-like condition in Col. Van Heusen, who is attacked by the creature. Mary Royce, who performs an autopsy on one of the men killed by the creature, says that "every ounce of edible fluid in his body is gone." Eric Royce comments that "It has to kill us or starve."

As in the other American horror films discussed here involving a vampire or a vampire-like creature, the creature in *It!* is repulsive. It is a humanoid reptilian creature with pig-like nostrils. It lives according to instinct. Thus, *It! The Terror From Beyond Space* places the vampire figure within the framework of evolutionary and disease concerns. Eric speculates that the creature is a devolved version of the Martian. After some disaster, "Martians, what was left of them, went back to bar-

barism." Thus, the creature is merely trying to survive by feeding on humans and has no motivation but pure survival instinct.

Ultimately, this film, like *First Man in Space*, uses the vampire figure as a warning against rapid scientific advance. Because the space race has accelerated too rapidly, humans travel to planets without knowing what vampiric horrors may await them there. At the end of the film, a spokesman for the space program tells reporters that Mars is "a planet so cruel, so hostile," that it will have to be bypassed in the journey of space exploration. "Another name for Mars is death!" the man tells the reporters, and, on that note the film ends.

While *The Horror of Dracula* and *The Brides of Dracula* were able to tap into the mythic sexual allure of vampirism, American cold war films were mired in imagining supernatural threats as historically specific ones related to fear of the Soviet Union and rapid technological advance. In a country in which political rhetoric had constructed the Soviet Union and its allies as the embodiment of all evil, all the terrors of the supernatural became connected with a specific ideology. Richard Hofstadter outlines cold war paranoia as a re-defining of the historical as the mythological. Hofstadter argues that in the climate of postwar paranoia, "History *is* a conspiracy, set in motion by demonic forces of almost transcendent power, and what is felt to be needed to defeat it is not the usual methods of political give-and-take, but an all-out crusade" (29).

Thus communism stands not as a historically specific political system but as an embodiment of mythological evil—pagan and satanic. The postwar Soviet Union becomes mythologically great and evil. I. F. Stone astutely commented during the 1950s that American liberals and conservatives alike painted communists as "some supernatural breed of men, led by diabolic masterminds in that distant Kremlin, engaged in a satanic conspiracy to take over the world and enslave all mankind" (69). Within such a climate the demonic threat of Dracula can only effectively be imagined within the framework of cold war politics. By contrast, and perhaps due to the less fervent anti-communist feeling in British films of the period, Dracula could reclaim his connection to the erotic. Even though the cold war threatened to erase Dracula's allure in American culture, he would, of course, rise again. American films such as *House of Dark Shadows* (1970), *Dracula* (1978), and *Love at First Bite* (1978), and *Bram Stoker's Dracula* (1992) would revive the count in all his erotic glory for a United States no longer confined within the rigid parameters of cold war fantasy.

Both British and American horror films of the fifties also imagined the evil Other of Communism within the guise of an exotic and Eastern threat, an Other that combined anxieties associated with the ancient East with concerns over contemporary politics.

4

THE EVIL EAST IN FIFTIES HORROR FILMS

The horror genre has typically drawn on images from a supposedly evil East to create its atmosphere of fear and danger. Stock characters such as the mummy, the gypsy, and the genie invoke the East as a place of mystery and danger. Specific horror works, beginning with the first Gothic novels, established the East as a suitable setting for frightening occurrences, as works such as William Beckford's *Vathek* (1786) and Horace Walpole's *Hieroglyphic Tales* (1785) indicate. The nineteenth century effectively refashioned the East within the context of British Imperialism: novels such as Richard Marsh's *The Beetle* and Bram Stoker's *The Jewel of the Seven Stars* (1903) used it as a means of conveying anxieties regarding imperialism and the Eastern Other. The classic Universal horror films of the 1930s and 1940s, such as *The Mummy* (1932) and its sequels, and *Cat People* (1942) and its sequels, linked supernatural occurrences with Eastern culture.[1] In the 1950s, horror films refashioned the ongoing association of the East with evil that was part of the genre within the framework of cold war concerns. Both American and British horror films from the 1950s use the East as a space to create a seductive evil that is related to the West's fear that the evil East's ongoing transformation would make it turn communist.

In his seminal work, *Orientalism*, Edward Said has argued that nineteenth-century Europe used the imperial Other as a locus for sexual fantasy and for all that threatened the supposedly logical organization of the British Empire. The use of the East as a space for fantastic scenarios of sexuality and evil served specific political purposes. European imperialism portrayed totalitarian governments as evolutionarily lower than and hence seeking enlightenment from democratic forms of government. Edward Said discusses European imperialism's perception of oriental despotism as "irrational, depraved (fallen), childlike, 'different,'" and therefore in need of parenting from European democracy (40). While World War II and the years immediately following it witnessed the final breakdown and demantling of the British Empire, much of the rhetoric of imperialism was absorbed into cold war rhetoric, including attitudes and perceptions of the East.

As Laura Nader discusses in her article dealing with the impact of the cold war on the discipline of anthropology, anthropological study as a handmaiden of British Imperialism was gradually giving way, in the Middle East, Far East, and Africa, to a new role as handmaiden of anti-communist American political interventions. Nader comments that "Neocolonialism replaced older varieties of colonialism, with the United States as leading power" (117). Yet, those in universities who tried to criticize this use of anthropology for overt political purposes were labeled as communists themselves: "Academic research began to focus on colonialism, but concepts of neocolonialism or U.S. imperialism were aggregated and presented as communist propaganda. Appeals to anti-communist propaganda obfuscated the reality of U.S. imperialism" (117). Further, as Nader points out, while anthropologists studying areas seen as vulnerable to communist take-over were given ample research funds, funding for study of the Soviet Union itself was denied, "as if it were somehow unpatriotic to know the enemy" (130-31). Thus the true evil Eastern influence (The Soviet Union) was left unknown and was represented largely through the repertoire of Eastern stereotypes drawn from imperialism. In her study of McCarthyism, Ellen Schrecker notes that "by the twentieth century, the American 'Other' had become politicized and increasingly identified with communism, the party's Moscow connections tapping in conveniently with the traditional fear of foreigners" (10).

In cold war Western perceptions of the Soviet Union there are elements that are similar to the characterization of the East by the British during their imperial dominion. As Said notes, one stereotype of the East prevalent during the nineteenth century was that it was a degenerated culture that now had become backward. Schrecker observes that one of the reasons that Americans were shocked by the Soviet explosion of an atomic bomb was because they perceived the Soviets as backward; hence, spy hunts had to be instigated, because, without espionage "how was it possible for the Soviet Union, which was viewed as a backward, barbaric nation, to have built a bomb?" (32).[2] As Robert Griffith notes in his study of McCarthyism, the appeal of the movement existed partly "because the Truman Administration itself couched its policies in a rhetoric of crusading anti-communism, which stressed American innocence, Soviet depravity, and the necessity for confrontation" (57). In an article published in *Social Text*, William Pietz has argued that cold war emphasis on the totalitarianism of the Soviet Union generates an image that consists of "nothing other than traditional Oriental despotism plus modern police technology" (58). Pietz maintains that one reason anti-Soviet cold-war rhetoric was so powerful and effective was because it "mapped certain traditional Orientalist stereotypes onto the Russians" (69).

While many propaganda films from the time period, such as *Invasion USA* (1952) and *Red Planet Mars* (1952) draw on an Orientalist repertoire to demonize the Soviet Union, horror films engage the oriental and demonic aspects of communism in a more complicated way. Horror films of the 1950s frequently fuse the threat of the demonic in communism with powerful manifestations of sexual allure.

In his notes that accompany the text of his anti-McCarthyist play, *The Crucible*, Arthur Miller argues that one thing the American 1950s and seventeenth-century Salem had in common was a tendency to link the demonic with the sexual: "Sex, sin, and the Devil were early linked, and so they continued to be in Salem, and are today" (35). Miller specifically links this sexualization of evil with American perceptions of the Soviet Union, stating that although the morals of the Soviet people are puritanical, "in American eyes at least, there remains the conviction that the Russian attitude toward women is lascivious" (36). Similarly, the Soviets view Americans as sexually corrupt and are shocked "at the very idea of a woman's disrobing herself in a burlesque show" (36). It is this very linkage between the enemy and a demonic sexuality that provides fascination: "Our opposites are always robed in sexual sin, and it is from this unconscious conviction that demonology gains both its attractive sensuality and its capacity to infuriate and frighten" (36).

Miller's commentary on anti-communism and its connection to a tendency in Christian society to conflate sexuality and demonology finds theoretical expression in other thinkers in the postwar world. Bataille theorizes eroticism through its inextricable connection with the demonic. For Bataille, the experience of erotic love is one that is bound up with fear: "The image of the loved one appears, first of all, with a precarious brilliance. It illuminates and at the same time frightens the one who follows it with his eyes" (*Visions* 228). According to Bataille, desire is frightening because it is an experience akin to demonic possession: "Possessed by desire, the individual is denied further recourse to exchange or transaction. Desire throws identity into turmoil: you cannot buy your way out" (Hollings 209). As Rodolphe Gasché notes in his commentary on Bataille, with regard to desire "Attraction through what inspires horror is its inevitable condition" (173). Fred Botting and Scott Wilson argue, in their introduction to *Bataille: A Critical Reader,* that in Bataille's works "jouissance is approached as the evil that it is, and embraced in its darkest forms, taking experience beyond every boundary, transgressing every law" (1-2). In Bataille's writings, he argues the association between the demonic and the erotic is one that is endemic to Christian culture. Further, he posits eroticism as horrifying as a universal within human experience. Yet while Bataille argues that the link between eroticism and the demonic has universal currency, the terms within which he couches this association have very specific historical resonance.

Bataille views eroticism as a force that opposes the state. Moreover, in the language that Bataille uses to discuss the nature of eroticism, it opposes the capitalist state in particular. Bataille asserts that "The truth of eroticism is treason" (*Erotism* 171). Seen within the context of the cold war, Bataille's writings suggest that the subversive and evil nature of eroticism could easily be associated with the threat of communism.[3] And, indeed, propaganda films such as *I Married a Communist* (1950) do make a strong association between erotic allure and the Soviet Union. Horror films from the same time period make this association as well, but frequently combine the elements of the evil East, communism, and eroticism.

Thus, for example, Universal Studio's *Cult of the Cobra* (1955) uses the alluring, yet evil, East as its central metaphor. The film deals with six American Air Force soldiers—Paul Able, Tom Markel, Carl Turner, Rico Nardi, Pete Norman, and Nick Hommel—who are stationed in Asia at the end of World War II. They meet a snake charmer, Daru, who says that if they pay him he will get them into a secret meeting of the Lamians. They sneak in and witness a beautiful woman's transformation into a cobra. Nick, however, tries to take a picture of the proceedings, and a fight ensues. Nick escapes with the cobra, but is bitten by it. While Nick is recovering in the hospital, the cobra returns and kills him. The other men return to New York, but the cobra follows them in the form of a beautiful woman named Lisa. She begins systematically killing the other men, but is hindered by her growing attachment to Tom. Finally Tom flings her, in cobra-form, out a window, and she dies.

The setting of the film is deliberately vague, but has the appearance of being India. At the beginning of the film we are merely told that the setting is Asia. The geographical uncertainty as to where the Eastern threat comes from is typical of Orientalism. According to Said, Orientalism relies upon making "an ontological and epistemological distinction . . . between 'the Orient' and (most of the time) 'the Occident'" (2). Thus, in Orientalism, the East is set up as a monolithic category that serves as the defining other of the West. During the nineteenth century, Western European culture's production of the East took place in literary, military, religious, scientific, and social discourses and action, and resulted in European culture gaining in strength and identity "by setting itself off against the Orient as a sort of surrogate and even underground self" (3), resulting in the view of the East as Other, a view which persists in twentieth-century Western society. The conflation between different Eastern cultures that typified nineteenth-century Orientalism is present in *Cult of the Cobra*. The soldiers see a veiled woman as they walk in the market, a detail that suggests Islamic culture, as does Lisa's clothing when she is in Asia. The snake charmer invokes Indian culture. The market and the emphasis on ancient goddesses invoke Egyptian culture. At the Lamian festival itself, the male participants engage in Russian-style dancing. The film creates an amalgamation of cultures that is labeled Asia—read: mysterious and dangerous.

The most obvious connection is, however, with India, a connection that in the 1950s was associated with a fear that, after gaining independence from Britain, India might be susceptible to communism. Nader notes that government funding for anthropological study in India was increased substantially in the 1950s, due to the perception that India was "a subcontinent also perceived as capable of sliding toward communism" (130). In India, *Cult of the Cobra*'s American soldiers foolishly pursue the forbidden by attending the Lamian meeting. The threat follows them to America, and, especially in the relationship between Lisa and Tom, indicates that the ideas of the East easily hold sway over impressionable Americans. For many anti-communists, the American perceived to be at risk for conversion to communism was the naive and trusting one. J. Edgar Hoover, in testimony given before HUAC, commented that he "would have no fears if more Americans possessed the zeal, the fervor, the persistence, and the industry to learn about this menace of Red fascism," and went on to express fear that liberals, progressives, ministers, school boards, and parents had been "hoodwinked and duped into joining hands with the communists" (119). Politically and culturally naive is exactly what the characters are in *Cult of the Cobra*. Yet, it is only in the guise of the erotic that the threat from the East can take hold of them.

The use of a beautiful Lamia as the seductress of the soldiers casts the Eastern threat in a sexual mode. The film has already portrayed the American soldiers as being weak due to their interest in the forbidden. Instead of concentrating on going home, they desire to know secret things about Asia—a curiosity that gets most of them killed. Before they go to the temple, they sit in a café getting drunk, a condition that produces their reckless behavior. Erotic allure proves to be more powerful than politics. Bataille argues that "The world of lovers is no less *true* than that of politics. It even absorbs the totality of life, which politics cannot do" (*Visions* 229). Thus, while the men in the film should be vigilant against a foreign threat both in Asia and in the United States, they are remarkably susceptible to it.

Even though he has just lost his fiancée, Julia, to his roommate, Paul, Lisa immediately entrances Tom. Lisa first appeals to him by moving in next door, then screaming in the middle of the night that she has been attacked by a man. Tom comes to her rescue and offers to show her New York. Even though Tom's dog senses that there is something amiss with Lisa, Tom never questions her presence and availability. When he asks her into his apartment and shows her a picture of his war buddies, he is offering them up as victims to her wrath. At a party given by Carl, Tom becomes jealous when Lisa flirts with Carl. However, she returns after the party and forces Carl to jump out of his apartment window. The film cautions against the American man's susceptibility to the alluringly foreign. Although Lisa does not appear particularly "Eastern" in any stereotypical way, it is some kind of Oriental quality in her that makes her attractive to the men she encounters, and her effect is degenerative. Daru says snake charming a cobra is "like looking death in the face." Lisa holds the same dangerous power over the American men she encounters.

The only character who is not powerless to Lisa's evil influence is Paul. The film suggests that it is his knowledge of Eastern culture that protects him and makes him wary of it. When the other soldiers laugh at Daru, Paul does not. He is a research assistant to a university professor and has heard of the Lamian cult before. Although Julia upbraids Paul for his belief in the cult—"Paul, you used to be so sensible!"—his belief in a mysterious, unseen, yet frightening threat gives him the strength to battle it. Like communism, the threat of the Lamia sneaks up on one unwittingly. For Hoover, communism was "the virus" that was "a menace to freedom, to democratic ideals, to the worship of God, and to America's way of life" (119). Lisa's covert threat, hidden beneath a beautiful exterior, is both the ancient threat of the mysterious East allied with the threat of the duplicitous woman, and the more recent threat of communist infiltration: the enemy within that succeeds through seduction. Only Paul's knowledge of the evil of the foreign culture allows him to expose the threat for the insidious thing it is—a cobra in the shape of a beautiful woman. Like Apollonius in Keats' "Lamia," the scholar defeats the snake woman. In *Cult of the Cobra,* the defeat is a fact to be celebrated, not lamented.

Man Beast (1956) presents a similar scenario of American innocence in the face of a dangerous and animalistic Eastern Other. The film concerns Connie Hayward's search for her brother, who is part of Dr. Eric Erickson's search team looking for the Yeti in the Himalayan Mountains. Connie, with the help of guide Steve Cameron, discovers that the most popular guide for expeditions in the region, Varga, is a Yeti himself who has been attempting to breed out the animal in his group of people by kidnapping human women and mating Yeti with them. Varga dies by falling from a mountain while chasing Connie and Steve to stop them from revealing his secret.

Like *Cult of the Cobra*, *Man Beast* uses an Indian setting to reference an untrustworthy and animal-like evil. Varga has been duping American expeditions by taking them in search of the Yeti and stealing the women who are part of the expedition in order to create a harem of American women to mate with the Yeti. The fact that the Americans naively fall into the trap illustrates the innocence of Americans in contrast to the corrupt nature of the Easterner. Erickson, an American scientist specializing in evolutionary studies, trusts Varga completely. Further, he holds an idealistic view of the Yeti. Erickson stresses the similarities between the Yeti and the humans, telling Connie that the Yeti are not covered with fur, but with "a hair quite similar to our own." Erickson dismisses the views that the Yeti may be dangerous, stating that "they're probably just simple people." Thus, instead of perceiving the danger of the Eastern Other, one that conceals an evil nature, the American adopts a naive and optimistic view with regard to the foreign. When Varga reveals his true identity to Erickson, he is horrified, labeling Varga as evil: "You're a devil, a devil incarnate." By then, however, it is too late, as Varga shoots Erickson dead.

As in *Cult of the Cobra*, the Eastern threat is one that threatens through deceptiveness, evil, and sexual threat. The question that the narrator poses at the beginning of the film with regard to the Yeti—"The question is always the same. Are they man or beast?"—is answered in the course of the film. The Eastern threat is animal. Like Lisa, whose beauty conceals a snake underneath, Varga has only the appearance of being merely a helpful guide. For Erickson, Varga fabricates a history of his life, claiming that he is the product of an American serviceman stationed in Calcutta and "a mountain woman with Mongol blood." In the film the animal side of Varga equals the Eastern side of him. When he reveals his true identity to Erickson, he wears an Asian-style silk jacket. Prior to murdering Erickson, he expresses Eastern views of the afterlife: "Goodbye, doctor, perhaps we'll meet again in some other incarnation." Varga's primary threat, however, is his kidnapping and raping of American women. While Lisa seduces Americans with her beauty, Varga violently kidnaps and rapes American women in order to breed the animal out of the Yeti people. When he relates to Erickson his plan to kidnap Connie, he comments that "Our offspring should be most interesting."

Like *Cult of the Cobra*, *Man Beast* reveals the dangers of naive Americans trusting an Eastern Other that conceals evil underneath, and this evil, the duplicitous of an East that is potentially turning communist, is cloaked in a sexual threat. While fifties American horror films like *Cult of the Cobra* and *Man Beast* focus on the naiveté of Americans in the face of a complicated and foreign threat that holds an allure, British horror films of the same decade approach the East differently, yet with a similar suspicion of the Oriental.

The onset of the cold war heralded the end of the British Empire, and no event more poignantly illustrated the demise of that empire than the Suez crisis of 1956. While the British perceived themselves as players in the cold war scenario that pitted an Egypt perceived, due to ties with Czechoslovakia and the Soviet Union, as growing closer to communism, and more antagonistic to the allies, the intervention of the UN, which forced the evacuation of British and French troops due to threats of Soviet intervention, signaled the end of Britain's dominating influence in the Middle East. The revival of the mummy in Hammer Studio films in the late 50s meant that the ancient mystery and threat of Egypt would from then on be perceived within the context of the cold war, with the 1950s-60s Middle East as one more potential battleground between communism and capitalism.

Hammer films revived the Orientalism associated with the British Empire, but did so in a world in which Orientalism had been absorbed into cold war rhetoric. *The Mummy* (1959) represents Hammer's retelling of the classic Universal mummy films. The film focuses on the Banning family, a family of archaeologists from Victorian England. During an expedition to Egypt, Stephen Banning, aided by his son John, finds the tomb of an Egyptian princess named Ananka. Stephen enters the tomb, screams, and develops a condition that causes him to be ruled insane. He is committed to a nursing home in England. Mehemet, an Egyptian priest of the god Karnac, brings the mummy of Kharis, a priest who loved Ananka, to England to get revenge on the desecrators of the grave. The mummy kills Stephen. He also kills Joseph, John's uncle, who has also been part of the expedition. The mummy then attempts to kill John, but John's wife, Isobel, stops him by using her striking resemblance to the princess to entrance him. The mummy kills Mehemet in order to save Isobel, and is subsequently shot multiple times, and then, apparently dead, sinks into a bog.

The Mummy represents nostalgia for the glory of the British Empire, nostalgia heightened by Britain's recent exclusion from the theater of Middle Eastern politics. The 1895 setting of the opening sequence highlights John's dedication to the pursuit of knowledge for the glory of the British Empire. Even though he has broken his leg, John refuses to leave the dig site and return to base camp. He ends up with a permanent limp, but shows dedication to the twenty-year search for

Ananka's tomb. The film expresses nostalgia for the British Empire's dominion over the East, represented in its subjects' ability to pursue profit and knowledge through archaeological research. Yet, like its Victorian, Orientalist predecessors, the film focuses on the danger of British intervention into foreign, especially, Eastern, cultures.

As the film unfolds, the desire to know and control the Eastern Other unleashes evil on England. While in Egypt, John says of the tomb, "there's something evil in there . . . I feel it." Stephen, after being committed to the Engerfield Home for the Mentally Disordered, warns his son about "the mummy who lives" and who "hates us for desecrating the tomb of its princess." The fear of reverse imperialism expressed in *The Mummy* makes this film an imitation of the Victorian Gothic and its Orientalist fantasies.[4]

Yet, within the context of the then recent Suez crisis and its concomitant fear of Nasser capitulating to communism, the threat of the world of Ancient Egypt overlaps with the fear of modern Egypt. One popular Orientalist stereotype common to the British Empire and to cold war politics was the notion that Eastern countries were incapable of progress. Immanuel Wallerstein argues that in the mid-twentieth-century "Oriental studies was based on the not-too-hidden premise that the high civilizations they were studying were frozen historically, that is, that they were incapable of proceeding autonomously to modernity" (198-99). In the flashback sequence that details Ananka's death, the totalitarianism of ancient Egypt is dwelt upon at length. As Pietz argues, cold war fear of totalitarianism was largely based on a perception of the "capacity for irrationality and contradiction in the communist-Oriental mind based on a lack of all sense of the truth of objective reality" (60).

Over one hundred people are put to death at Ananka's funeral, a detail that emphasizes a lack of concern for individual human life amongst the Egyptians. One popular stereotype about the East and about communism was that both displayed a lack of concern for human life. In a personal account posted on the Korean War Project web site, George Matta discusses his experiences as a prisoner of war in terms of a lack of respect for human life and individuality. Matta and other men in the camp "fight with our bare fists to keep the Commies from undressing the dead"; to their horror, they discover that the Chinese have dug up all the dead, stolen their clothes, and left them in the open. Matta then comments, "*If this is communism, and I think it is, they can have it.*" While the Egyptians in the film decry grave robbing, they venerate an ideology that encourages reckless expenditure of human life. Further, the brutal punishment handed out to Kharis when he transgresses the law—having his tongue cut out and being buried alive in a secret tomb—revives stereotypes of Oriental cruelty common to both British imperialist and anti-communist rhetoric.

In a confrontation scene with Mehemet, John reveals the Egyptian's barbarity and backwardness. Mehemet protests that "I'm a civilized man. To me the dead are the dead," but readily admits "In my country, as you know, violence is commonplace." John accuses Mehemet of worshipping a "third-rate god" (Karnac), and thus arouses the priest's fury and reveals the evil totalitarian who lurks beneath the veneer of the civilized gentleman. Yet, as in *Cult of the Cobra*, these political ramifications are played out against the backdrop of the erotic and its interconnections with the political demon of communism.

In *The Mummy,* erotic attachment both abets and challenges the totalitarianism represented in the worship of Karnac. Kharis' transgressive love for Ananka allows the cult of Karnac to strengthen. A fundamental point Bataille makes in his discussion of transgression and taboo is that transgression always reinforces the taboo it appears to violate. Within Bataille's thought transgression never represents simply a subversion of the dominant order. Thus, while the taboo stands as a limit that makes the act of transgression attractive, so the act of transgression reinforces the power of the taboo. Ultimately, however, the mummy's continuing love for Ananka, even in the form of her physical double, Isobel, inspires him to defy Mehemet, and eventually kill him when he orders the mummy to murder Isobel. As in *Cult of the Cobra*, the erotic serves to disguise evil ideology in an attractive package—Ananka is reckoned to be the most beautiful woman in the world—but, also, may frustrate totalitarianism with desire that is stronger than politics. Hammer's follow-up to *The Mummy* also displays British horror films' concerns with the instability of the Middle East during the cold war.

Curse of the Mummy's Tomb (1964) focuses on a British expedition in search of the tomb of Ra-Antef, son of Ramses VIII. The expedition successfully locates the tomb, but enrages the Egyptian government when the American backer of the expedition, Alexander King, decides to create a traveling sideshow featuring the mummy and the other antiquities. Meanwhile, Annette Dubois, a member of the expedition falls under the spell of a wealthy British man, Adam Beauchamp. The mummy disappears from King's possession and soon begins killing those involved with the expedition. The mummy is revealed to be under the control of Adam Beauchamp, who is really Be, the brother of Ra-Antef who has been condemned to eternal life after murdering his brother three thousand years ago. Be wants Annette to spend eternity with him and orders Ra to kill her and him both. Ra refuses to kill Annette, but kills Be, and then destroys himself.

Like *The Mummy, Curse of the Mummy's Tomb* displays both nostalgia for the British Empire and concern with its collapse. In the 1900 setting of the film the British possess the top archaeological minds and possess the morality to handle the relics properly. For example, Sir Giles Dalrymple deplores King's plan to put the mummy and other antiquities on display. Giles labels King's plan as "childish exhibitionism." King ruins Giles' reputation and proceeds with his plan. Thus, while the British have the morality and brains to lead and succeed in the expedition, anxiety about the influence of American money is prevalent in the film. King is completely motivated by financial concerns, and because he holds the purse strings, he can control what happens to the antiquities. Just as postwar Britain felt resentment towards America's wealth and demands that Britain repay the U.S. war loans, Giles and the other members of the expedition feel resentment toward King's materialism.

Further, King's confidence illustrates a lack of American diplomacy with regard to Middle East politics. King expresses stereotypical views of the Egyptians that enrage Hashmi Bey, the representative of the Egyptian government. King comments about Hashmi that "they're all alike. Always getting into a stew about something." When Hashmi accuses King of sacrilege in his exhibition of the mummy, King retorts "Nothing sacrilegious about making money." When King watches a native dancer in an Egyptian restaurant, he comments to her, "You ever learn to do that to ragtime, give me a call. We'll make a fortune." Even though King's callous attitude toward the Egyptians enrages the government, his suspicions about Hashmi are proven to be correct. The British, such as John Bray, another member of the expedition, are taken in by Hashmi's cooperation with them, when in reality he is an ardent worshipper of the mummy and despises archaeological attempts to take antiquities from his country.

Thus, as in *The Mummy*, British imperialism is under siege from an untrustworthy and superstitious Middle East. Yet, this film also acknowledges the threat from American money as being as powerful as the unstable East in taking away British political influence. The mummy may kill many members of the expedition, but American money has already killed British influence and power before the mummy ever rises from the tomb. Further, the film points out the ineptness of Americans in handling their newfound influence in the East. King cannot recognize the real threat that Hashmi and his anti-Western sentiment conceal, but rather only see him as an "inscrutable" buffoon. The fact that the mummy kills King first indicates the carelessness of his handling of the East.

Horror films of the 1950s drew on Orientalist stereotypes of the evil East common to the genre and overlaid them with a fear of communism as constituting the latest degenerative form that the totalitarian East was assuming. Within the guise of the erotic the East is alluring—a lamia, an Egyptian princess—but dangerous to the Westerners who succumb to the spell. For the United States, emerging in the 1950s as the new defender of freedom in the East, the allure of the East comes in the form of a living woman or man who dupes naive Americans. For Britain, aware of its loss of influence in the sphere of Middle-East politics, it comes in the form of an alluring dead princess and her dead lover, or in the form of an ancient mummy summoned from the grave by his brother.

While the dangerous foreign Other maintained a clear demarcation in fifties horror films between them and us, other horror films of the period broke down that distinction by showing the monster within the domestic and supposedly safe world of home.

Hitchcock's masterpiece *Vertigo* engages issues of eroticism and horror, causing the characters to travel a fine line between life and death. Courtesy of the Library of Congress.

Vincent Price, king of the B-horror film, and star of such horror classics as *The Fly*, *The Tingler*, and *House of Wax*. Courtesy of the Library of Congress.

Philip Wylie, father of the notorious concept of Momism. Courtesy of Library of Congress.

Vlad the Impaler, real-life inspiration for Dracula. Courtesy of the Library of Congress.

Cold war standoff, a cartoonist's imagining of Kennedy-Khrushchev conflicts. Courtesy of the Library of Congress.

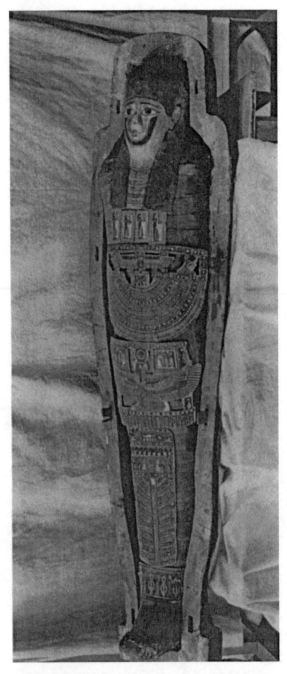

The ancient Egyptian mummy continued to be a figure of fascination in cold war horror films like *The Mummy* and *Curse of the Mummy's Tomb*. Courtesy of the Library of Congress.

J. Edgar Hoover, director of the FBI and prominent cold war rhetorician. Courtesy of the Library of Congress.

Anthony Perkins as Norman Bates, key cold war horror character who speaks to the fear of loss of self. Courtesy of the Library of Congress.

Alfred Hitchcock on the set of *Psycho*. Courtesy of the Library of Congress.

Part III

Horror in the Home

HORROR OF THE LONELY CROWD:
CONFORMITY AND FIFTIES HORROR FILMS

For Bataille, eroticism and the world of work are always at odds with each other. The social world that demands work and production always tries to limit eroticism, which is the expression of reckless expenditure. Bataille comments that "Lovers, in any case, tend to negate a social order that contests more often than it grants their right to live . . . love is itself an opposition to the established sacred order . . . in the same way that the individual's being is at odds with social reality" (*Accursed* 159-60). Bataille's opposition between the personal and erotic and the work world became a hot topic in cold war social commentary. Both American and British horror films of the period deal with a fear of conformity that the work world creates and opposes the horror of conformity with the realm of the erotic. This chapter traces the dialectic between work and love in several horror films from America and Britain.

One central fear that plagued Americans in the postwar decade was the fear of conformity. Adam Wolfson argues that "what most disturbed the fifties social critics was the bogy of conformity. They believed that the American people were becoming ever more alike." While the fear of conforming found fictional expression in mainstream 1950s culture in such works as *The Man in the Gray Flannel Suit*, this fear also took shape in horror films.

The most influential of fifties sociological studies of a mutating American character is to be found in David Riesman's *The Lonely Crowd*. Along with his two collaborators, Reuel Denny and Nathan Glazer, Riesman sought to define a change taking place in the American personality. The book appealed more to a mainstream audience than to an academic one. As David Webster notes, by 1995 *The Lonely Crowd* had sold 1.4 million copies, which was "over twice as many as those sold by any other work of sociology written by American and Canadian sociologists who were alive in 1995" (66). The popularity of the book resulted in Riesman, in 1954, being the first sociologist to appear on the cover of *Time*. The success of the book arose from its tapping into a deep-seated fear in American audiences.

In *The Lonely Crowd*, Riesman discusses the historical development of three personality types. The first personality type is what he calls "tradition-directed." This type flourished during precapitalist Europe. In this society, "the culture, in addition to its economic tasks, or as part of them, provides ritual, routine, and religion to occupy and to orient everyone" (11). The next personality type, "inner-directed," emerged during the Renaissance and Reformation. Riesman comments that "*the source of direction for the individual is 'inner' in the sense that it is implanted early in life by the elders and directed toward generalized but nonetheless inescapably destined goals*" (15). For the inner-directed man, choice, no longer the purview of social organization, is channeled through "a rigid though highly individualized character" (15).

Riesman believed that the inner-directed man was in decline in postwar America. An emergent personality type known as the "other-directed" man was gradually supplanting him. The other-directed man looks for direction not to internal traditions instilled early in life, but looks to friends and to the mass media as guides for his behavior. Consequently, "*the goals toward which the other-directed person strives shift with that guidance: it is only the process of striving itself and the process of paying close attention to the signals from others that remain unaltered throughout life*" (22). This other-directed man was an object of horror for many Americans of the fifties.

The Lonely Crowd's popularity stemmed not so much from the subtle nuances of its sociological analysis, but because it created an appropriate bogeyman for the decade. As Wilfred McClay argues, Riesman and his collaborators "may well have intended to write a neutral description and analysis" that even affirmed some of the aspects of the other-directed personality, "but the public embraced *The Lonely Crowd* because they found it a great secular jeremiad against other-direction" (41). McClay goes on to argue that the book was particularly successful because Riesman was a sage "dressed, not in the black robes of the Protestant minister, but in the more respectable business suit of social science" (41). Whether readers simplified Riesman's message or not, they responded to a new figure of horror, one that sprang from a society moving toward an eerie conformity.

The conformity facing the fifties man was one that raised questions about what constituted proper postwar masculinity. If wartime society demanded physical and psychological bravery as tests of manhood, what did the conformist work world of the 1950s ask of men? The role of breadwinner husband and father characterized men of the decade. Barbara Ehrenreich notes in her studies of fifties masculinity that "If adult masculinity was indistinguishable from the bread-winner role, then it followed that the man who failed to achieve this role was either not fully adult or not fully masculine" (20).

Yet, in order to be the breadwinner, the fifties man had to enter into a work world that seemed to threaten his manhood. A mechanized work world seemed to pose the danger of robbing men of their masculinity in the very act within which they were forced to prove themselves as men. As Andrew P. Hoberek argues, while postwar families benefited from the economic booming occurring in the middle class, men "also underwent the structural proletarianization of being forced to sell their mental labor and to perform work that was becoming . . . as alienating and rationalized as factory labor" (376). Thus the work world offered fifties men the paradox of being "on the one hand agencyless, conformist drones, or the other secure possessors of masculine authority" (379-80). Sociologically, the fear of conformity focused primarily on men. While Betty Friedan would paint a similar portrait of feminine conformity in *The Feminine Mystique*, fifties horror films focused on bizarre transformations of working men into inhuman monsters.

The Amazing Colossal Man (1957), a sf-horror film, tells the story of Lt. Colonel Glenn Manning, an army officer who is exposed to the blast of a new type of nuclear weapon. Because he tries to save a pilot who has crashed into the test site, Manning runs into the test area and is hit directly by the blast. Although he has third-degree burns over one hundred percent of his body, he survives. Even more miraculously, he begins to grow more skin. Problems arise as he begins to transform into a giant. His new skin cells are growing at an accelerated rate. While the doctors try to help him, and Manning's fiancée, Carol Forrest, attempts to comfort him, Manning falls prey to physical and mental illness. Eventually he breaks out of the army compound and moves toward the city of Las Vegas, striking terror into the city's inhabitants, until the army shoots him, and he falls into Boulder Dam.

The Amazing Colossal Man is fraught with anxieties concerning the bomb and masculinity. In an act of masculine bravery, Manning attempts to save the downed pilot, yet this act of courage does not make him a big man socially, but, rather, literally makes him a big man. While one of the measures of masculine confidence in the 1950s was height—as *The Amazing Colossal Man*'s brother film *The Incredible Shrinking Man* highlights—Manning's state of transformation becomes a cruel parody of height.[1] He grows eight to ten feet a day, loses his hair, and is forced to wear a sarong that resembles a diaper. Manning does not look like a big man, but, rather, like a big baby, an idea highlighted by his constant rages and crying fits. Manning puzzles over why he has been transformed into a monster, "a circus freak," as he refers to himself: "What sin can a man commit in a single lifetime to bring this upon himself?" When Manning meets with his fiancée, Carol, he mocks his previous ambitions by recalling that in his college yearbook he was voted "man most likely to reach the top," then laughs bitterly. When Manning treks through the Las Vegas strip he takes a giant crown off the top of one of the casinos, eyes it close, then rejects it, knowing that he is not king, not really a big man(ning), but a victim of a powerful military organization.

Anxieties concerning transformation and masculinity are also present in the film's portrayal of the military power structure's rejection of Manning. Manning risks his life in the line of duty, yet military officials deny responsibility for what has happened to him.[2] When his doctors approach the officials at the base the officials refuse to recognize any connection between the transformation of Manning and the plutonium-bomb blast he has been exposed to. The officials try to separate Manning from his fiancée, Carol. A security officer from the Nevada site visits her in the middle of the night and tells her she can no longer see Manning in the hospital. In flashbacks, we learn that the military has defined Manning's life and also called upon him for sacrifice. He volunteers for the Korean War, postponing his marriage to Carol. The bomb test that transforms him takes place on the very day he is to finally wed her. As Manning's doctors fight to find him and inject an antidote into his bone marrow in order to stop the growth and save his life, military officials threaten to kill him. Manning's situation is much like the real-life situation of the naval soldiers present at the Bikini tests or the marines who participated in atmospheric bomb tests in Nevada.[3] His very manhood hinges on his ability to face the threat of nuclear weapons bravely, yet those weapons threaten to take away his manhood and, eventually, his life.

War, the military structure, and finally nuclear weapons rob Manning of the ability to be a man with a private life. In this sense, *The Amazing Colossal Man* charts not only the transformation of 1950s masculinity due to the new technology of nuclear weapons, but, also, the fear of loss of humanity that many associated with a world faced with a radical new technology. In the film, cold war politics invade the realm of the personal, as the postponement of Carol and Manning's wedding indicates. Instead of marrying in Las Vegas as they have planned, Manning is transformed into a giant who terrorizes the city, and Carol must watch him, helplessly, a victim of his deteriorating mental condition and of a security state that wants to hide from her the effects of nuclear weapons.

Many in the fifties feared dehumanization and looked to the personal realm as a means of counteracting a society increasingly numbed by new technological discovery. Lewis Mumford emphasizes the personal as an antidote to a dehumanized and dehumanizing society bent on nuclear destruction (60-61). Riesman also sees the fear of the dehumanization of sexuality and the personal realm as a factor producing anxiety among the lonely crowd (154).

In the sequel to the film, *The War of the Colossal Beast* (1958), dehumanization defines what has happened to Manning. In this film, he is discovered in Mexico to be an inhuman monster. Half of his face is dead, as the empty eye socket and exposed bone indicate. Even the change in title, from *Man* to *Beast*, suggests how his character has altered from victim of fallout to a monster that has to be hunted down. He has lost the ability to speak, although he does remember his former life. When he commits suicide by electrocution, we see the final transformation of Manning: someone who starts out as a successful military officer has become a hideous monster who must kill himself.[4]

Thus, conformity leads to dehumanization and degeneration. If a man follows the dictates of the organization, he will end up monstrous. In this sense, *The Amazing Colossal Man* and the two films I discuss below, chart fifties readers' responses to *The Lonely Crowd* as a work embodying "nostalgia for the lost American virtues of self-reliance and rugged individualism" (McClay 42). Manning's act of bravery in trying to save the individual pilot should make him a hero, but in an other-directed world, it makes him a monster.

Another fifties horror film, *Monster on the Campus* (1958), also uses the metaphor of monstrous transformation to examine issues of conformity and individuality. It focuses on strange happenings at Dunsfield University, occurrences that stem from Dr. Donald Blake's bringing a newly discovered species of fish to the campus for study. Blake's student Jimmy Flanders inadvertently allows his dog, Samson, to drink the fish's blood, and thereupon the dog transforms. Then, Blake accidentally cuts his finger on the fish's mouth and he begins transforming into a caveman, going on to kill a nurse, his bodyguard, and a forest ranger, and then attempting to kill his fiancée, Madeline Howard. He does these things without knowing what he is doing: does them in periods of blackout. When Blake realizes that he is the killer, he begins experimenting on himself, discovering that the fish's plasma mixed with gamma rays has produced the transformative substance. He makes himself undergo a final transformation, then allows the police to kill him.

Monster on the Campus adopts the typical sf/horror plot of the mad scientist versus blind authorities, but frames this issue specifically within the world of the organization man. William Whyte's 1956 book *The Organization Man,* like *The Lonely Crowd,* was a sociological study that resonated with popular audiences. Whyte laments the encroaching ability of organizations to take over every aspect of a man's life. He comments that "group–relations advocates have been saying, it is the whole man The Organization wants and not just a part of him. Is the man well adjusted? Will he remain well-adjusted? A test of potential merit could not tell this; needed was a test of potential *loyalty*" (172). Dunsfield University is just such an organization that demands all of Donald Blake. When Blake brings a prehistoric species of fish to the campus, the president of the university, Dr. Gilbert Howard, sees no scientific value in the discovery. He focuses on what the fish means to the organization as a whole. He tells his daughter, Madeleine, that because "every paper in the country" ran the story of the fish it will "pay off one thousand percent in alumni donations." When Madeleine asks him about the scientific merit of the fish, he gives her a lecture in which he says, "an organization is like a living organism." Blake gives himself entirely to the organization, working long hours routinely. However, once he begins putting forth ideas that threaten the organization, yet express his individual scientific research, the university perceives him as a threat.

As Whyte laments, by favoring conformity the organization stamps out individuality and its own ability to thrive. He argues that the personality tests that routinely began to determine employee viability in the fifties were "loaded with values, organization values, and the result is a set of yardsticks that reward the conformist, the pedestrian, the unimaginative—at the expense of the exceptional individual without whom no society, organization or otherwise, can flourish" (182). When Blake puts forth his theories about regression in order to explain the murders that are taking place on campus, he is correct, but he angers Dr. Howard and a colleague, Dr. Cole, both of whom conspire to have him put on leave. While Donald lectures to his students that man can "choose the direction" his evolution will take, the university conspires to stamp out individuality that does not follow the direction of the organization as a whole. The last straw for Dr. Howard is ultimately a financial one. When he learns that Blake has made an eighty-eight minute phone call to Madagascar for research purposes, he intervenes in order to stop Blake's research.

While the film pits Blake's inner-directed man against the organization, it also reveals that a specter of the other-directed society can be found in women. Blake's fiancée, Madeleine, is a spy for the organization. While he wants her to support his theories, she reports to her father, Dr. Howard, that Blake has been dismissing his classes. Further, she is the one who reveals that he is making the phone call to Madagascar. Within fifties debates about conformity and individuality, women were sometimes seen as abating the transformation of the United States into an other-directed society. Largely because of women's age-old association with the role of socializer, women were seen as a threat to masculine individuality. Fifties nostalgia for individualism replayed a typical myth of United States culture, the frontier myth. Within these myths, as Nina Baym argues, "the encroaching, constricting, destroying society is represented with a particular urgency in the figure of one or more women" (72). Blake's impending marriage to Madeline means that even at home he will be forced to conform to the organization's standards, not only because she will domesticate him, but also because she will serve as a spy for her father's interests.

Blake's flight to a cabin in the woods to willfully transform himself into a caveman illustrates the frontier myth as the basis of his desire for individuality. But, if the film condemns the other-directed society as stifling scientific knowledge, it equally condemns Blake's rampant inner-directed man. It reveals, in fact, that the individual within is a beast. Thus, when Donald willfully transforms himself, stating that "As a man, this possibility terrifies me, but as a scientist I must learn the truth," his individuality is revealed to be a slavishness to the ideals of science. Much like the university's insistence on organizational conformity, Blake's scientific purism sacrifices the man. Whtye argues that the organization should ask for the worker's best effort, but "not ask for his psyche as well" (201). Blake has given Science, if not the organization, his soul.

While *The Amazing Colossal Man* and *Monster on the Campus* trace the threat of organizational society to the work world, another fifties horror film ultimately locates the dehumanizing organization mentality within the home. *The Alligator People* (1959) tells the story of Joyce Webster's search for her missing husband. On their wedding night, her husband, Paul, after receiving a telegram, mysteriously leaves the train they are on. Joyce finally traces Paul to Bayou Landing, a small town in Louisiana. At a plantation there, which Joyce's believes is Paul's home, Joyce encounters Mrs. Hawthorne, a woman who denies knowledge of Paul, but eventually reveals herself to be Paul's mother. Along with Mark Sinclair, a scientist, Mrs. Hawthorne has put Paul under experimental treatment for wounds he has received as a result of a plane crash during his military service. Sinclair has used alligator glands to treat burns. While the treatment has been initially successful, all the patients, including now Paul, have transformed into a half-human, half-alligator form. Paul convinces Sinclair to try a radical treatment on him using gamma rays from a cobalt bomb. The treatment fails, however, and Paul transforms into a beast with an alligator head and torso but human legs. He dies by sinking into quicksand on the bayou.

Like *The Amazing Colossal Man, The Alligator People* locates dangerous conformity in the military world. After both Joyce and Paul have served in the Korean War, they expect to attain domestic happiness once they are discharged. Joyce draws attention to the fact that they have had to postpone their marriage: "Why did we have to wait so long?" Joyce asks Paul as they sit happily in the train compartment. When the couple reads congratulatory telegrams, Paul comes across one that disturbs him and causes him to get off the train, abandoning Joyce without an explanation. In voice-over narration Joyce laments "It was supposed to be the happiest day of the life . . . but I'd just seen my husband's face for the last time." Initially, the film makes the audience believe that the military structure has reclaimed Paul and taken him away from the domestic happiness he has been promised in postwar life. As the film unfolds, however, we see that the conformist structure responsible for his transformation into inhuman monster is really the home.

One concern about postwar men's inability to reach mature manhood was centered in the fear that they would never be able to break away from the controlling and dehumanizing power of their mothers. In a world in which popularized Freudian psychology began to hold sociological currency, the dominating mother frequently assumed the sinister guise usually afforded to the corporate or military official who robbed men of their individuality, making them into other-directed zombies.[5] While, as David Riesman has commented in a recent article, the American Dream of the 1950s was "in several senses of the word a domestic dream" (342), sometimes the domestic realm, which should have provided a haven from the pressures of the conformist work world, was perceived as a place of conformity itself.[6] Nowhere did the fear that mothers were creating emasculated conformist sons find more eloquent expression than in the writings of Philip Wylie.

Wylie's "Common Women," an article that appeared in his book *Generation of Vipers,* introduced the concept of Momism into American society. Wylie perceives the cult of Momism as a degenerative one that harms American men. In the article he blames mom for World War II and compares her desire to control and manipulate American culture to Goebbel's propaganda campaigns (215). In annotations added in 1955 to the original article, which was written in the forties, Wylie refuses to back down from his fear that mom is producing a country of conformists. He states, "The nation can no longer say it contains many great, free, dreaming men. We are deep in the predicted nightmare now and mom sits on its decaying throne—who bore us, who will soon, most likely, wrap civilization in mom's final, tender garment: a shroud" (196).

In these annotations he links the security state of the Cold War to the dominance of Momism in the United States: "The enemy explodes uranium, plutonium, hydrogen; still they absurdly cry, 'Keep these things forever an American secret—for security's sweet sake. Peace, peace, peace! A great victory for momish 'thinking'" (217). While Wylie's statements are clearly extreme, Momism held currency in fifties America and was one of the forms of conformity feared by American men.[7]

Paul's transformation from military hero and new husband into alligator-man occurs because of his mother's desire to exert control over him. When Joyce first visits Mrs. Hawthorne, Mrs. Hawthorne displays complete and utter hatred for her, believing that she has no right to know what has happened to Paul, and even going so far as to lock Joyce in her bedroom. Lou Ann, Mrs. Hawthorne's servant, tells Joyce that "this is a trouble house." The trouble has come from Mrs. Hawthorne. We soon learn that she has pressured Sinclair to try the experimental treatment on Paul that has resulted in his transformation. Instead of being able to share this horrible secret with Joyce, he can only tell his mother and even wishes Joyce gone: "She's got to leave on that morning train tomorrow." When Paul enters his mother's mansion, he walks up to a chair believing his mother sits there and asks, "Mother, has she gone?" When he realizes that it is Joyce who is sitting in the chair, he runs, unable to face his wife because he is so under the power of his mother's influence.

Mrs. Hawthorne's demanding personality results in Paul being unable to assume mature sexuality and remaining perpetually childlike: she also represents a threatening conformity in that she wants him to remain forever entrenched in the bayou country where he was born. When Paul pleads with her, "Why didn't you just let me die?" she responds by caressing his face. In the plane crash Paul has been involved in, his injuries have resulted in a face that is "completely gone. Horribly burned." Yet, by allowing his mother to use him as a guinea pig he has become not just literally faceless, as finally his human face transforms completely into an alligator's face, but completely dehumanized. Yet, even in his final transformed state, he is still mom's drone. After breaking free from the table where he has been receiving the radiation treatment he turns first to his mother, then to Joyce. Even in the grip of his non-human hatred his mother is his first choice. When the swamp swallows Paul up at the end of the film, he has been completely assimilated into the maternal Southern culture represented by Mrs. Hawthorne.

Whether it is the work world or the world of mom threatening to make the American man give up his individuality, horror films of the period tell their audiences that conformity will win, but at the price of a monstrous dehumanization. Whether these films featured giant, cave man, or alligator, these metaphors spoke for American anxiety that post-war men were losing their humanity in the face of encroaching group thinking at home and at work. Unlike the compromise that a film like *The Man in the Gray Flannel Suit* strikes between Tom Rath's individualism and his role as breadwinner, American horror films of the decade suggest that no such compromise is possible.

Fear of work-influenced conformity also finds expression in British cold war horror films, but the focus seems to be more explicitly on how mass thinking via the media is posing a danger to the personal and erotic. Much social criticism in 1950s Britain focuses on the massification of culture via popular entertainment and housing estates. As P. Yvard comments, within British art, "The postwar hero deeply resents the dangers of a modern society thwarting the development of culture . . . soon after the second world war, the individual is taken in an unavoidable succession of selections and rejections connected with his education and his professional life and social class" (41). Coupled with the loss of Britain's status as a world power, fear of an encroaching massification in British society provoked horror.

Horrors of the Black Museum (1959) focuses on a popular journalist, Edmond Bancroft, who writes sensationalized accounts of murders in London. Gradually, the film reveals to the audience that is Bancroft himself who has been staging the murders in order to have subject matter to write about. Through injections, he has made his secretary, Rick, into a mindless drone who carries out the murders for him. When Bancroft forces Rick to kill his own fiancée, Angela, Rick loses control and reveals Bancroft as his master. The police shoot Rick dead as he is completing the act of stabbing Bancroft to death.

Bancroft's victims illustrate the way the film opposes Bancroft's obsessive work with eroticism and the personal. His first victim, Gail Dunlap, is killed by a pair of binoculars that contain knives in them that she receives in the mail. Gail and her roommate Peggy are excited by the gift, believing it to be from one of Gail's male admirers. When the police question Peggy, they suspect one of Gail's boyfriends as being behind the murder. When Bancroft deals with his next victim, his mistress, Joan, the film strongly highlights his association with a world of work that stifles the erotic. Joan is being kept by Bancroft, but she disparages his manhood, suggesting that their relationship is not a sexual one. When they argue, Joan tells Bancroft, "Without your money, you'd be no man at all." Joan tells Bancroft to leave because "I'm going to find myself a man. A real man. A whole man." Joan celebrates her freedom from Bancroft by dancing in a local pub and flirting with the men there. In a conversation that she has with the bartender, Tim, she tells him that she wants to have fun because her parents worked hard all their lives, never went out, but were killed by a bomb during the war. "I'm going to have fun. I'm going to live," Joan tells Tim right before she goes home and is decapitated by Rick, working as Bancroft's drone. Bancroft's opposition to the personal finally results in his downfall as his order that Rick kill Angela causes the scheme to be revealed to the police.

The film portrays Bancroft's obsession with his work to be insanity. Bancroft seems to spend all his free time at the police station, taunting the police and trying to get classified information about crimes. Bancroft's doctor, Dr. Ballan, tells him that his obsession with his work is wrecking his health: "Cut down on your work and learn to relax." Ballan eventually diagnoses Bancroft as having psychiatric problems. The doctor goes to Bancroft's house to talk to him, and Bancroft kills him by electrocution. The film suggests that a maniacal devotion to work leads to horror. Rick, Bancroft's mindless drone, reinforces this idea. Rick never has time to go out with his fiancée, and when Bancroft allows Rick to take her to a fun fair, it is only for the purpose of having her killed.

It is not just work per se, however, that the film is concerned with. Bancroft's particular profession, true-crime author, indicates the film's concern with the massification of society. While arguing with Bancroft, Superintendent Graham accuses him of writing "without much conscience." When Bancroft signs autographed copies of his latest book in a bookstore, a man upbraids him for corrupting the man's teenage son. Bancroft's burning desire to write sensationalized books and articles that appeal to a mass audience results in him becoming a murderer. As Superintendent Graham says at the end of the film, "He created a reign of terror so he could write about it."

A Hammer hybrid of horror and science fiction also indicates British culture's fear of a mass force stamping out individualism. *X: The Unknown* (1956) focuses on a series of mysterious deaths. All the victims have radiation burns, yet there is no plausible explanation for the burns. However, Dr. Adam Royston, an American scientist working at a British lab, traces the deaths back to an unexplained fissure that has appeared on a British military base during a radiation safety drill. As the mysterious force in the fissure grows, it leaves the fissure and begins claiming victims outside the military base. To stop the force Royston uses a device he is working on to neutralize atomic bombs.

In the film, the strange force that feeds on radiation and kills is totally mindless—it operates by pure instinct. As Royston posits, the force must feed on radiation to survive and simply moves toward radiation sources, killing people mindlessly in the process. In a country increasingly concerned about mass culture after the war, the mindless blob may be read as allegorizing the mass mind. British social critic Richard Hoggart, in *The Uses of Literacy*, condemns mass publications because of their tendency to create a mass mind that makes individuals incapable of thinking for themselves. Hoggart comments that "The price paid for this [massification] in popular reading is that a small group of imaginatively narrow and lamed publications are able to impose a considerable uniformity" (196). The force, a mindless blob of mud, suggests a visual image of a culture increasingly losing individuality. This idea is further underscored in the film by the way in which the force interrupts and destroys the erotic and the personal.

As Bancroft's obsession with work is placed in opposition to the personal in *Horrors of the Black Museum*, *X: The Unknown* opposes the mindless destruction of the force with scenes of the erotic and personal. One of the force's victims is a lab technician. He has gone into the radiation lab of the hospital in order to have a romantic rendezvous with a nurse. They begin kissing, and the technician exclaims, "Why didn't we start doing this earlier?" Immediately, he hears a strange noise. He goes into an enclosed chamber of the lab and encounters the force, which melts the skin off his body. The nurse suffers from such a severe case of shock that, as her doctor says, "she won't be able to tell you her own name." Another victim of the force is a young boy, Willie Harding, who is badly burned by the force, slips into a coma, and then dies. After the boy's death, Royston attempts to comfort Harding's father. But the father turns on him saying, "you meddle with things that kill. You're not safe. You're a murderer."

Like many sf/horror films, *X:The Unknown* points the finger at science for creating a society threatened by a lack of individualism.[8] Lewis Mumford, for example, feared that the postwar paranoia in the countries possessing nuclear weapons would result in Nazi-like experimentation on citizens, leading to "the worst sadism" disguised as "responsible scientific experimentation with live subjects" (*Sanity* 30). He foresaw a future in which "radioactive water has become the ideal medium of mass extermination" (*Sanity* 68). As Royston makes clear, it is the presence of large quantities of radioactivity on the earth's surface that has called forth the force in the first place. Hence, in *X: The Unknown* the mindless work world of science threatens to kill the erotic and the personal.

Cold war horror films from both the United States and Britain illustrate a fear that the post-World War II work world is encroaching on everyday life and destroying the personal and erotic. Whether it is the mass media, controlling mothers, science, the military, or any number of other everyday forces, cold war horror charts an intense fear that the personal was disappearing and giving way to a society of drones.

Fifties horror examined and questioned the supposed safety of the domestic as a haven from the external threats of cold war politics in other ways as well.

6

DOMESTICITY AND HORROR

Locating the scene of horror within the family has long been a staple of the genre. From the creature's strangulation of Elizabeth on her wedding night in Mary Shelley's *Frankenstein* to Damian's murderous tricycle ride in *The Omen*, the domestic has provided an effective stage for the invasive power of the horrible Other. Bataille's opposition between the world of work and the erotic and violent Other that threatens that world can also be understood through a Freudian framework. Most typically, the horror of the domestic has been understood within the framework of Freud. Indeed, horror and Freudian interpretation have long been thought of in tandem. Freudian theory has proved an especially useful hermeneutic device when discussing postwar horror films, due to the popularization of Freud that pervaded fifties American society. To discuss the fifties family, whether in sociological reality or in fictional representation, usually requires engaging popularized theories drawn from Freud, such as the Oedipus Complex. However, British horror films from the same time period tend to be less infused with Freudian symbolism and theory than do American ones. British horror films frequently highlight how horror at the domestic level could come to be generated in the form of class transgression. In this chapter, I will examine both American and British horror films in order to explore the different guises of the horrific within the realm of the domestic.

The popularization of Freudian theory in fifties America was typically used as a means of diagnosing what was wrong with the domestic situation in America. Thus, films as diverse as *Rebel without a Cause*, *Psycho*, and *Pillow Talk*, trace abnormalities in human behavior back to unresolved Oedipal conflicts. In an important way, Freudian theory was used in fifties America to construct widely accepted notions of normality especially within the realms of marriage, sexuality, and childrearing. Discussing Lionel Trilling's appropriations of Freud in the 1950s, Mark Krupnick argues that fifties intellectuals attempted to drain Freud of any subversive potential in order to make him a voice for conformity to their society's norms: "Thus there emerged in the fifties a revision of Freud's thought which stressed adjustment, adaptation, assimilation, and acculturation" (270). Far from being perceived as a threat to 1950s' domesticity and normality, Freud was fashioned as one of the staunchest supporters of these notions.

In *Freud: The Mind of the Moralist* (1959), Philip Rieff constructs a Freud whose ultimate lesson promotes conformity to society as it is. Paramount in Rieff's book is the image of Freud as a devoted husband and father, a normal man who charted the abnormal territory of the mind, but only in order to reinforce the importance of normality itself. Rieff says that "Freud's life was in no sense great. He behaved well, married late, died in his own time full of honors and years" (xxv). Rieff is particularly concerned with Freud's discussions of sexuality. Rieff seeks to defend Freud's theories against those who believe that they sanction sexual license. Rieff argues that "Least of all did he hope for the sexual revolution with which some misinformed people have linked his name" (xxiii). Rieff's Freud is one who endorses monogamy and marriage: "Freud considered sensuality without affection a degrading state of affairs, and set forth his conception of 'a completely normal attitude' in love and marriage as fusion of tenderness with sensuality" (179). Although Rieff credits Freud with "unearthing the sexual daemon beneath," he sees the value in Freud's theories in the fact that Freud always remained "far from admiring instinctual revolt" (309). According to Rieff's study, Freud weighs in on the side of what would come to be fifties norms regarding marriage and sexuality.

In other important ways, Rieff constructs a Freud for America. Thus, he links Freud's rising popularity in the United States to his rejection of revolutionary political stances. By offering "a brilliant formula with which to shrink the revolutionary character—as basically in revolt against his father" (267), American society can embrace a Freud who is ideologically congruent with anti-communism.

Most of all, for Rieff, Freud's importance for American society lies in the morality that he offers in the form of a thinking man's conformity. Because Freudian theory forces the individual to resign himself or herself to a constant inner war between id and superego, it causes the individual to accept things as they are: "his is not a therapy of belief but one which instructs how to live without belief" (334). Rieff's Freud is similar to Trilling's Freud, one who "reconciles man to his unhappy fate . . . a Freud whose sole power is to console" (Krupnik 279). Fifties culture created a Freud who brought authority in order to reinforce its views of normality.

In an article entitled "Why Horror? The Peculiar Pleasures of a Popular Genre," Andrew Tudor argues that attempting to generalize about horror is a fruitless activity. He argues that the question should not be "why horror" but "rather why do *these* people like *this* horror in *this* place at *this* particular time? And what exactly are the consequences of their constructing their everyday sense of fearfulness and anxiety, their 'landscapes of fear' out of such distinctive cultural materials?" (461). For American horror films of the period, popularizations of Freud provided a powerful means for the genre to explore its own obsession with social normality.

Much criticism of the horror film focuses on the transgressive nature of the genre, and, frequently, horror films are about transgression. Critics as diverse as Barbara Creed, Harry M. Benshoff, and Mark Jancovich explore the transgressive nature of horror films. Interestingly, the domestication of Freudian theory also opened the door for horror films to be about normality. An example of how cold war horror could use the abnormal as a means of defining and reinforcing the normal is *House of Usher* (1960).

House of Usher is a reworking of the Poe classic "Fall of the House of Usher." In Richard Matheson's screenplay, the nameless narrator of Poe's story is transformed into Philip Winthrop, the fiancé of Madeline. He has come to Usher to claim her for his bride. Philip encounters opposition from both Roderick Usher, Madeline's brother, and Bristol, the butler, who lives in the house. Roderick tries to convince Philip that Madeline is a member of a family line that is cursed, and that therefore she should neither marry nor have children. Philip continually rejects this notion. Madeline wants to leave with Philip, but Roderick pressures her to stay. Madeline apparently dies of heart failure after a fight with Roderick. Roderick places her in a coffin in the family crypt. When Philip learns from Bristol that Madeline has suffered from catalepsy, he searches for her, but she has left the coffin. Now insane, she attempts to kill Philip, but it is actually Roderick whom she kills, doing so as the house burns down due to flaming logs that have caused the carpet to catch fire during the struggle. As the house burns down, Philip escapes.

In his account of his filmmaking career, Roger Corman notes how psychoanalysis influenced his making of *House of Usher*. Corman says that at the time he made *Usher*, he "had begun reading a lot about Freudian psychology and the inner workings of the psyche" (77-78). He even went into analysis himself in order to learn more about Freudian theory. He maintains that his goal was "to use Freud's theories to interpret the work of Poe" (78). Thus, Corman's use of Freud illustrates the social dynamic of the film: the dialectic between normality and abnormality so dear to 1950s interpretations of Freud.

In the film, Philip Winthrop embodies the rationalist morality that Rieff praises as being at the heart of Freud's thought. Philip intrudes on the house of Usher in order to claim Madeline for the normal world of marriage and family. The film opposes Philip to the abnormality of Roderick. In the first scene in which Roderick and Philip speak, Philip wears a blue suit and Roderick wears a long red jacket and has rouged lips. In comparison with Roderick's decadent appearance, Philip appears physically normal and healthy. When Madeline enters the room in a pink dressing gown, we see an image of gender normality—Philip in blue and Madeline in pink—the normal boy and girl with the normal desire to get married. Roderick's vehement objection to Philip is over the issue of marriage. "Are you actually planning to marry my sister?" Roderick asks Philip, showing his alienation from the normal world of heterosexual marriage that Philip wants to lead Madeline into.

Mark Jancovich argues that *House of Usher* creates sympathy for the outsider character of Roderick that challenges "notions of 'normality'" (278). Jancovich maintains that life with Philip would be so mundane that "the perverse relationship between Madeline and Roderick looks positively desirable" (279). Jancovich reads Corman's films as transgressive. I, however, believe that an interesting aspect of *House of Usher* from a psychological viewpoint is that it uses Freudian-inspired horror techniques to validate normality. Roderick is a fascinating villain, but scarcely a sympathetic one. As Gary Morris notes in his study of Roger Corman, Philip functions as a "vital character" who ventures into "a realm marked by images of death and decay" (95). In the film, as contrast to Roderick as "living corpse," Philip is the center of normality and identification (95).

Philip consistently adopts a common-sense attitude with regard to the strangeness of the house. Unlike Poe's narrator, who is attracted to that strangeness, Philip reacts to it in the way a fifties homeowner might, horrified that Roderick would allow Usher to fall into such dilapidation: "Don't you think that crack in the wall should be repaired?" Roderick and Bristol assume a fatalistic attitude toward the house. Bristol tells Philip, "If the house dies, I shall die with it."

Specifically, Philip rejects the notions of heredity as destiny that Roderick puts forth. As Tony Williams notes in his study of the family in horror films, psychiatric theories stressing the importance of heredity in human behavior were regarded as "reactionary" in the 1950s (87). As Krupnick notes, even the orthodox Freudians of the fifties tended to stress adaptation as a result of previous tendencies toward "overestimation of the cultural factor" (269). Consequently, normal and rationalist viewpoints were ones that rejected biological factors in favor of social ones. Thus, Philip tells Roderick that he doesn't believe in "the sins of the fathers being visited on the children." Philip labels Roderick's belief in supernatural and hereditary factors as abnormal: "I will not let your sickened fantasies destroy Madeline's life."

House of Usher transforms Poe's romantic tale of self-destructive love into a tale of normal, heterosexual lovers impeded by a sexual pervert. In D. H. Lawrence's essay on Poe in *Studies in Classic American Literature*, Lawrence argues that Poe romanticized self-destructive love: "Doomed he was. He died wanting more love, and love killed him. A ghastly disease, love. Poe telling us of his disease: trying even to make his disease fair and attractive. Even succeeding" (42). If Poe romanticized the incestuous love of Roderick and Madeline, Corman's film rejects this love as perverse.

As is typical of American movies of the time aimed at a youth audience, in them the older generation embodies the abnormality that prevents the kids from attaining normal domesticity. David Hogan argues that *House of Usher* appealed to teen audiences because Matheson's script recast Roderick as her father so it played on generational conflict (212). While Hogan believes that the film portrays the father as trying to suppress "her youthful sexuality" (212), I see the opposition as more between the abnormal corruption of the older generation and the normality of the younger generation. Teen horror films such as *Monster on the Campus* (1959), *The Giant Gila Monster* (1958), and *I Was a Teenage Werewolf* (1957) all locate their characteristically frightening abnormality in older authority figures.

Corman's film highlights Roderick's unnatural love for Madeline. As Morris observes, in the film, "the closest thing we see to a marital relationship is between Roderick Usher and his sister Madeleine" (90). Upon arriving at Usher, Philip demands to see Madeline, but Roderick tells him, "She is confined to her bed." Roderick addresses Madeline with a fondness that is altogether too strong to be appropriate for a brother, "my dear." When Philip sneaks into Madeline's bedroom to kiss her, Roderick intrudes. As Roderick is showing Philip the portraits of the Usher ancestors, he lasciviously points out the Usher women's propensity to become harlots. Philip's dream reveals to him most strongly Roderick's abnormal desires for Madeline. Roderick carries a white-clad Madeline over the threshold and smirks at Philip, who tries to stop him. Madeline's coffin is her wedding bed, and when Philip tries to free her, she screams, a scream that bleeds into her real screaming as Philip wakes up.

Corman likens the house of Usher to a woman's body and the explorations of the house to an adolescent boy's curiosity about that body, stating, "The deeper you go into the dark hallways, then, the deeper you are delving into, say, an adolescent boy's first sexual stirrings" (80). What Philip discovers as he explores Usher in search of Madeline is an abnormal deflowering. Philip lingers over the blood-stained coffin, and his hands keep touching Madeline's blood as he searches for her. Madeline hides her mad eyes behind her bloodstained hands, screams, and then strangles Roderick, who whispers to her, "There was no other way. No other way." Even if Madeline's blood represents Philip's anxiety about deflowering her, his desire is the normal desire of a fiancé, whereas Roderick's incestuous love is abnormal and brings about death and destruction.

Thus, *House of Usher* reflects fifties America's use of Freudian theory to construct a stable notion of normality. Unlike Poe's narrator, who gets "infected" by Roderick, Philip remains apart from Roderick's madness, and, even if he cannot save Madeline from Roderick's abnormal love, he can leave the ruins of Usher behind.

Another horror film from the period also uses an explicitly Freudian metaphor in order to explore the disruption of domestic normality. *The Tingler* (1959) focuses on Dr. Warren Chapin and his experiments regarding the physiological reactions the human body experiences when in a state of fear. Chapin discovers the existence of an insect-like creature he names the tingler when an acquaintance of his, Oliver Higgins, brings the dead body of his deaf-mute wife, Martha, to his laboratory. Because Martha could not scream, she has died of fright. Warren subsequently discovers that Oliver has murdered his wife for her money. He brings the tingler back to Oliver's house in order to put it in Martha's body and discovers a mask and other trappings that Oliver has used in order to frighten Martha. The tingler gets loose in the movie theatre that Oliver owns, but Warren and Oliver retrieve it and put it back in Martha's body. The tingler then reanimates Martha's body causing Oliver to die of fright.

The Tingler places a great deal of emphasis on domestic strife as the backdrop for the discovery of the strange creature produced by fear. Warren is enmeshed in a troubled marriage with Isabel, a promiscuous woman who is openly unfaithful to him. Isabel's sister, Lucy, tells Warren of Isabel that "she's out every night, and with men that aren't very nice." Warren watches the next morning as Isabel returns at one a.m. and kisses a man on their doorstep. Isabel's failure as a wife is compounded by the fact that she has murdered her own father in order to get his money. Further, she produces domestic strife in the film by trying to impede normality by blocking the marriage of Lucy and David, Warren's assistant. Warren urges her to allow Lucy to marry, stating, "They're nice kids. They're in love." Like Roderick in *Usher*, Isabel represents a degenerate force that attempts to block domestic normality.

The Freudian associations between the tingler and the blind instinctual demands of the id are borne out through Isabel and her use of the tingler as a murder weapon against Warren. Upon first viewing the tingler, Isabel is drawn to it and its "tremendous power," as Warren describes it. Isabel pretends to want to be a "new" and good wife and offers a reconciliation with Warren. Warren makes a direct connection between Isabel and the tingler, stating "I hope the new wife doesn't turn out to be as dangerous as the tingler." Isabel subsequently drugs Warren's drink and unleashes the tingler on him. He is saved by Lucy from being strangled by the tingler. The tingler stands as an external representation of Isabel's id, the force that destroys not only her domestic life with Warren, but her father's life and her sister's hopes for happiness.

The film mirrors Warren and Isabel's troubled marriage in the marriage between Martha and Oliver. Oliver immediately expresses bitterness that Martha owns the silent-movie revival theatre that they run together. Further, Martha is a scold and a penny-pincher who trusts no one and eventually drives Oliver to kill her by frightening her to death. When Oliver tries to justify the murder of Martha to Warren, he tells him that he doesn't know what such a marriage is like. Warren replies that "I know exactly how it was, Ollie." Like Isabel, Oliver follows the dictates of his id and disrupts the domestic. The tingler frightens Oliver to death, indicating that he is punished by the force of the id that he has followed so blindly. Thus, as in *Usher*, instinctual perversion disrupts the domestic, indicating the dangers of veering away from the normality of home and family.

While *House of Usher* and *The Tingler* represent 1950s American horror's appropriation of Freudian theory to chart normality and abnormality within the domestic realm, British films from the same time period utilize a sociological basis to give us a portrait of the abnormal within the home. While American horror tends to explore the psychosexual dimensions of abnormality, *Village of the Damned* (1960) uses a class-based sociological perspective to explore abnormality vs. normality.

Village of the Damned, which is based on John Wydham's novel *The Midwich Cuckoos*, focuses on a mysterious occurrence at the village of Midwich. Everyone in the community falls asleep temporarily while the village is surrounded by a mysterious forcefield. Two months later, all the women capable of having children discover that they have become pregnant. They eventually give birth to healthy and perfectly formed babies who differ from normal children through their accelerated growth rate and high intelligence level. These special children form a closed group. When military officials discover that other villages have had the same experience, they contemplate destroying the children, but Gordon Zellaby, the "father" of David, the leader of the children, asks for a year's respite so that he can teach them. He discovers that the children have a collective consciousness. When the children begin killing other members of the village who threaten them, Zellaby agrees to destroy them along with himself by blowing up the schoolhouse in which he has been teaching them.

P. Yvard notes that one of the major sociological changes in postwar Britain was the development of a new type of man who through the use of his intelligence could move out of his working-class origins and join the middle class. Yvard notes that in the late fifties "Owing to advanced studies which the Welfare state allowed him to undertake, the postwar hero leaves his original class and marries into a higher one" (38). The "scholarship boy," as Richard Hoggart labels him in The *Uses of Literacy* (1957), was a new phenomenon in 1950s Britain and one that challenged class-based notions of intelligence.

While the scholarship boy seemed to demonstrate that high intelligence was a frequent occurrence among working-class people, and success attainable for them, the scholarship boy also functioned as a figure of abnormality, both for his own class and for the other classes. On one level, as Hoggart points out, many parents of working-class boys were suspicious that the scholarships they received would take them out of the norm of experience for people of their class: "Parents who refuse, as a few still do, to allow their children to take up any scholarships are not always thinking of the fact that they would have to be fed and clothed for much longer; at the back is this vaguely formulated but strong doubt of the value of education" (71-72). To his own parents, sometimes, the scholarship boy became abnormal. Similarly, he was never fully accepted by the members of the other classes. This caused him to view himself as abnormal, as someone who fit nowhere. As Yvard notes, "he himself goes on living in a sort of no man's land between the upper-middle class refusing to integrate him completely and the lower class with which he can no longer identify himself" (38).

Village of the Damned reflects concern about the abnormality of children who have become classless due to their superior intelligence. David's superior intelligence might be seen as natural due to the fact that his putative parents, Gordon and Anthea, are upper-class, but Gordon soon discovers that members of this special set of children who have been born to working-class mothers possess exactly the same levels of intelligence and skill that David possesses. Gordon teaches David to open an oriental puzzle box. He then visits a working-class home, that of the Harringtons, and discovers that the two special children there are capable of precisely the same feat. Indeed, while David is the leader of the children, the film makes a point of showing that many of the special children come from working-class homes. In fact, the film shows none of these special children coming from middle-class homes, and thus suggests that the village is comprised only of the wealthy Zellabys and a number of working-class families.

Part of the uncanniness of the children resides in their essential sameness, each one being in very many ways identical to his or her fellows. Moreover, Gordon discovers that they possess a collective consciousness. The children walk around the village in a pack, wearing black raincoats and similar clothing, just as scholarship children wore the same uniforms as the other students from different classes. The children of Midwich are oddly blank: they lack personality and differentiation. Yvard discusses the scholarship boy as one who loses his identity: "Gradually, his individuality happens to be crushed down through a loss of any sense of belonging. He loses his accent, his social background at an age when the main traits of his character have been shaped" (38). Hoggart also discusses a loss of individuality in the scholarship boy, who is perceived by society as having a "rather-better-than-normal intellectual machine" (243) and is "trained like a circus-horse, for scholarship winning" (244). In *Village of the Damned,* the children are pawns of a higher form of alien intelligence that has planted them on earth in order to take over the planet.

In the film, the villagers' reaction to the abnormality of the children differs according to their class. The working-class families are suspicious of the children. After the village has woken up from the sleep, Miss Ogle, a clerk at the grocery store, says the experience is "unnatural." When the children are born, one working-class father says, "I hope none of 'em lives." The working-class men continually pose a threat to the children, finally forming an angry mob that unsuccessfully attempts to burn the children up in their schoolhouse. James Pawle, who eventually becomes a victim of the children, speaks for the working-class men when he says of the special children, "They're not human. They ought to be destroyed." Ironically, while the villagers view the children as abnormal, physically they are completely normal. When Doctor Willers examines an X-ray of David prior to his birth, he says, "it is more than normal." The nurse who attends the delivery of David calls him "perfect."

If the working-class people in the film see the children's hyperperfection as abnormal, Gordon defends it, perceiving it to characterize the children's evolutionary superiority. Gordon argues with his brother-in-law that these special children have developed the way that they have as a result of their environment. He tells a panel of experts that "They may be the world's new people." He hopes that they may bring a better world: "Look at our world. Have we made a good job of it?" While events in the film increasingly challenge Gordon's view as the children kill more and more people, their intelligence remains framed in evolutionary terms: they kill for self-preservation. After learning that the Russians have obliterated an entire village in order to destroy the special children of that village, David tells his uncle: "We have to survive. No matter what the cost."

Village of the Damned complexly engages the social change in postwar Britain that created a new class of people. While the film shows the horror of children who are classless and without individuality, it also implies that from an evolutionary viewpoint they are superior. Hoggart describes the scholarship boy as one who "has moved away from his 'lower' origins and may move farther" (245). The film reflects the disease that society felt with a socially mobile child with superior intelligence. The film juxtaposes Gordon's admiration for the children with the working-class families' sense that the children are unnatural beings in their homes. The idea of the working-class intelligent child as freak is also borne out in the sequel to the film.

Children of the Damned (1963) focuses on a group of children from different countries who possess high intelligence, collective consciousness, and destructive power. When two British scientists, Tom Lewellin and David Neville, begin investigating the intelligence of the children, the children, led by a young British child, Paul, escape from their respective embassies and hole up in an abandoned church under the care of Paul's aunt, Susan Eliot. British intelligence services working with the military determine that the children should be exterminated after they kill several British military men who have gone into the church. Neville agrees with this assessment, but Lewellin attempts to save the children by asking them to go to their embassies. When the children do what he asks, they kill ambassadors and military men there who want to use the children's advanced intelligence to make new superweapons. The children go back to the church and are subsequently killed when a screwdriver drops on a machine and thus gives a false order to the military to fire upon the church.

Like *Village of the Damned*, *Children of the Damned* initially locates the problem of the children within a social-class context. When Neville and Lewellin realize the superior intelligence that Paul possesses, they immediately want to locate the parents. Neville comments that "Breeding tells," but when they visit Diana Looran, Paul's mother, they discover her to be a working-class prostitute who refuses to tell them anything about Paul's father. After Paul causes his mother to be hit by a car, however, she confesses to the scientists that she was a virgin when Paul was born. Neville, a geneticist, is puzzled by the fact of Paul's intelligence when there is no genetic basis for it. Lewellin, the psychologist, discounts Diana's profession that Paul "hasn't got a father. He isn't human." However, when Diana's words are proven true, the film, like *Village of the Damned*, attributes the superior intelligence of the working-class child to superhuman causes. And, again, this intelligent child is perceived to be a threat to the safety of the world. While *Children of the Damned* references the danger of the scholarship boy as its predecessor did, it also views this type of a child as a national asset.

The children come from various countries—India, Nigeria, the United States, China, Russia, and Britain—but Paul, the British working-class child, is the clear leader of the group. While the class level of some of the children is unclear, Lewellin comments that all the children were the product of "an unstable mother and no trace of a father." Even though they all score identically on the tests and share a collective consciousness, Paul is the undisputed leader of the group, suggesting a British fantasy of both the power and danger of the new breed of child in postwar Britain with both intelligence and education. Colin Webster, an intelligence agent who works on the mystery of the children, sees Paul as an asset to Britain, but simultaneously views him as a threat, finally sanctioning the murder of Paul along with the rest of the children. The duality of Paul as both asset and threat to Britain is further underlined by the lack of direction possessed by the children.

Hoggart's discussion of the scholarship boy as one trained to win prizes like a machine fits the children in the film. They possess great intelligence and power and band together, but they are unable to express to anyone their purpose for being on earth. When Lewellin goes to the church in an attempt to speak to the children and possibly save them from being killed, Susan Eliot, speaking for the children tells him that "They've been hunted like some kind of freak vermin." Lewellin then asks the children to explain to him their purpose. Paul answers, "We don't know." Even if, as Professor Gruber professes, the children possess "the cells of man advanced maybe a million years," they have no clear purpose for their existence. While they fight against being used as pawns in the arms race, they have no clear plan of their own, suggesting the displacement and danger of the highly intelligent, yet displaced, child who has risen to another level of awareness, but has no direction.

Whereas *House of Usher* and *The Tingler* locate abnormality in a perverse sexuality that denies heterosexual marriage and the normality of the domestic, *Village of the Damned* and *Children of the Damned* locate abnormality in the superior intelligence of a new race of children who defy their domestic surroundings. Thus these American films shows the American horror film looking to the family in order to diagnose the aberration there that prevents domestic happiness. By contrast, these British films show a Britain concerned with a new type of child emerging in the postwar period, one who defies class barriers. Both films show us that horror functions as a vehicle that registers social anxieties about what is normal and what is abnormal.

While *Village of the Damned* and *Children of the Damned* illustrate the fear that children may bring horror into the home, teenagers and women were often also perceived as potentially dangerous internal threats in cold war horror.

Part IV

Teenagers, Moms, and Other Monsters

7

MONSTER AT THE SODA SHOP:
TEENAGERS AND FIFTIES HORROR FILMS

The teenager is one of the most recognizable of the images of the 1950s decade. From James Dean, tormented in his screaming red jacket in *Rebel without a Cause*, to John Travolta, embodying a seventies' black-leather fantasy of the fifties teen in *Grease*, the images tell us what we all know: that the 1950s gave birth to teen culture. The sheer volume of teenagers seemed to demand that they have a culture of their own. Between 1946 and 1960 the number of teenagers in the United States increased from 5.6 million to 11.8 million (Clark 69). Yet, the increase of teenagers in America did not give rise to optimism about the future, but, rather, produced fear in Americans writ large as the increased numbers carried the danger of violence with them. The years 1948-1953 saw the number of juvenile delinquents charged with crime increase by forty-five percent (McGregor 22). The film industry became interested in the dangerous aspects of the teenage criminal, producing such films as *Rebel without a Cause* (1955). Yet another genre, which was equipped to deal with the horror of the new teen culture, also took advantage of the hot topic of the teenager. Fifties horror films, like *The Giant Gila Monster* (1959), *The Blob* (1958), and *I Was a Teenage Werewolf* (1957) use horror metaphors to explore a wide variety of issues related to the emergence of teen culture in postwar America.

The fifties teen was perceived socially as a figure of transgression. Like Bataille's lovers who threaten the everyday world of work and order with their passion, teenagers were perceived as a social threat because of transgressive desire. Gaile McGregor comments vis-à-vis teen culture and rock and roll: "Considering the context, in fact, we could almost say that rock and roll managed to combine the numen of the cowboy and the noble savage in one improbable package. And that's only the least of it. The real secret to the success of fifties rock . . . was sex." (24). While crime was the stated fear associated with juvenile delinquency, teen transgression was also typically linked with sexual transgression. Fifties America sought to find a solution to the problem of the troubled and transgressive teen by turning to authorities.

Juvenile delinquency provoked feelings of intense horror in people living in America at that time. Benjamin Fine found the title of his 1955 book *1,000,000 Delinquents* from his prediction that by the end of the decade the United States would be the home to one million teenage criminals. Fine's book, like other studies of delinquency published in the fifties, seeks to locate the causes of the delinquency problem. While commentators would find a variety of causes for this problem, the most central and disturbing one found it located in authority structures, and especially authority structures within the home. For Fine, the person who should be held accountable for the problem of juvenile delinquency is the father. Fine comments that "First of all, a child needs a 'father figure.' This means that he needs to identify himself with a person stronger and wiser than himself. Boys especially need to identify themselves with their fathers" (60).[1]

For Fine, as for other thinkers who tried to understand the social problem, the oedipal model that held the father accountable for his son's behavior also held accountable all the fathers of American society. Fine states that "If Billy 'goes wrong,' the finger of blame can be pointed in just one direction: at society—at you and me—for having given him no chance to 'go right'" (105). Fine's argument is congruent with the ideas of another commentator on delinquency, psychoanalyst Robert Lindner, whose book *Rebel Without a Cause* brought the concept of the teen rebel into American consciousness. Lindner believes that the rebellious psychopath derives his behavior from "a profound hatred of the father" (8). Also, like Fine, Lindner accuses not just individual fathers, but the fathers of society, the authority figures: "modern American society errs in failing to provide the kind of substitute for self-expression which in other times and other cultures drained off a considerable portion of behavior opposed to the best interests of most people" (14). If mainstream films like *Rebel without a Cause* finger the father as the cause of teenage angst, horror films frequently go further by locating the psychopathic disease not in the teenager at all, but in an external force, or, more frightening, within authority itself.[2] For horror films, authority frequently does not so much fail, but willfully creates monsters.

The Giant Gila Monster is a low-budget horror film set in Texas. It follows the experiences of Chace Winstead, a teenage boy who leads a very responsible gang of other teenagers. The sheriff has Chace aid him in an investigation of mysterious car accidents that begin with the disappearance of two of Chace's friends. Eventually, through the sheriff's and Chace's efforts, a giant Gila monster, which has mutated due to a thyroid condition, is found to be the culprit behind the disappearances. Chace devises a plan to kill the monster, which is impervious to bullets. He drives his hot rod, which is carrying nitroglycerin, into the creature and kills it.

The Giant Gila Monster works to exonerate teenagers from the label of juvenile delinquent by illustrating that they are the virtuous alternatives to authority figures who are at best clueless and at worst willfully corrupt. While the film seems to start on a note of condemnation of teen culture, as we see Pat and Liz, parking in the woods to neck, killed by the Gila monster, it soon changes tone and allows other teens to emerge as the heroic force in the film. The film sets up Chace as an ideal figure. He works at an automotive repair shop in order to support his widowed mother and his sister, who suffers from polio. The typical scene of the teens at the soda shop is the second sequence we see in the film and here, with Chace as their leader, they are seeking only good, clean fun. Chace brags to the sheriff that he has controlled the other teens, commenting that "Pat's the only one of the gang I couldn't slow down," and reminding the sheriff that Pat is the only one of the group to have gotten a speeding ticket, even though the boys' biggest obsession is souping up their hot rods.

The disappearance of Pat and Liz causes the authorities to suspect the worst of the missing teenagers. Their suspicion highlights a common fear associated with the emergent teen culture of the decade—sexual transgression. In Gabriel Almond's 1954 study of juvenile delinquency and its connection to communism, he perceives the desire to join the Communist Party on the part of American teens as linked with a rebellion against authority, and a rebellion that frequently took a sexual form. In a case study of a female teenager, he comments that "Joining the party made it possible for Frances to have sex relations, not because they gave her satisfaction, but because she could show contempt for the ordinary laws of society" (291).[3] The authorities in the film suspect sexual transgression at the base of the disappearance, when, in fact, what they should be looking for is a zoological mutation that no one can control. Pat's father, Mr. Wheeler, approaches the sheriff for help in locating his son, and the sheriff immediately suspects that the two young people have eloped, or worse, telling Wheeler that "If they were out together all night, you'd better hope they have [eloped]." The sheriff grills Chace, asking if Pat and Liz were in any kind of trouble, meaning sexual trouble. Chace denies this, but it continues to be the suspicion that motivates the sheriff's investigation. Thus, even though Chace continually helps the sheriff with his investigation, the sheriff remains suspicious of the motivations of teenagers.

The film goes to pains to illustrate that Chace and his gang are much more responsible than the authority figures who surround them.

Chace's relationship with the sheriff makes it clear that Chace is in control of the investigation, and, in fact, Chace does finally solve the problem of the Gila monster. Moreover, every authority figure he is opposed to comes off negatively in relation to him. His boss, Mr. Compton, does not know how to handle nitroglycerin, and Chace has to prevent an accident from occurring when Compton transports some to their garage. The DJ, Steamroller Smith, whom Chace admires, drives drunk and wrecks his car, resulting in Chace having to tow him out of a ditch. Even Chace's mother, whom he supports, criticizes him for spending too much time fixing up his hot rod, even though he is simultaneously providing admirably for her and his sister. Wheeler is the most flagrant example of malicious authority, as he abuses his position as wealthy oilman in order to influence the investigation and try to arrest Chace, because he irrationally blames him for Pat's disappearance. The final scene of the film illustrates Wheeler's recognition that Chace has solved the mystery. Acknowledging that he himself is a poor example of authority, Wheeler returns his deputy's badge to the sheriff and offers Chace a job.

Perhaps the most striking manner in which the film attempts to show teen culture as admirable, and not threatening, is through its portrayal of rock-and-roll music. In 1950s America, rock and roll was perceived as a threat that was related to the problem of juvenile delinquency. J. Ronald Oakely discusses the fear associated with teen reaction to "Rock Around the Clock," a song that appeared in the 1955 film *The Blackboard Jungle*. Oakley states that "All across the nation, public school principals and teachers held special meetings with town officials to try to determine how to handle the young when the movie came to their town, and some cities dealt with the problem by banning the movie" (273). In 1956, a psychiatrist testified that rock and roll was "cannibalistic and tribalistic" and encouraged wanton rebellion (Clark 69). The issue of race was paramount in many of these objections, such as one made by segregationist Asa Carter, who concluded that rock and roll "appeals to the base in man, it brings out animalism and vulgarity" (qtd. in Clark 69).

The Giant Gila Monster reframes rock and roll as a positive force in American culture. In one of the subplots of the film, Chace pursues a rock-and-roll career. Steamroller Smith helps him in his career and plays for the teenagers one of his recordings at the barn dance that is invaded by the Gila monster. The teens love his rock-and-roll song, but love equally a religious song he sings to them while strumming a ukulele. We have seen earlier in the film that Chace sings this song to his sister when she is learning to walk with her new braces. Thus, as the film argues, rock and roll is morally regenerative, not degenerative. The monster is outside, waiting to break in on the teenagers; it is not inside teen culture, as many perceived it to be.

The Giant Gila Monster, then, works to remove the taint of the monstrous from teen culture by making one threat to American society turn out to be a zoological freak of nature. The film removes the fear of a phantom threat that has been wrongfully associated with a culture that is admirable. One moral of the movie is that authority figures should learn to stop suspecting monstrous acts among teenagers and should look for the real threats in their society. Moreover, the film suggests that whenever possible authorities should use teenagers as their role models.

Another teen-horror film from the same time period also sets up teenagers as more vigilant than the adult authorities. *The Blob* focuses on Steve Andrews and Jane Martin, two teenagers who witness a meteor falling from the sky. While driving home, they pick up an injured elderly man who has opened the meteor and now has stuck to his arm a strange substance that was inside the stone. They take him to Dr. Hallen and go with other teenagers to investigate the site of the implosion. The blob absorbs the old man and then absorbs Dr. Hallen and his nurse. Steve and Jane go to the police, but the authorities refuse to believe in the existence of the blob. Steve and Jane sneak out of their houses and band together with other teenagers to find the blob. They locate it in Steve's father's grocery store and set off air raid sirens, blow their horns, and call the fire department in order to get the attention of people. The police are still skeptical until the blob invades the movie theater. Steve, Jane, Jane's brother, and others get trapped in the diner, and the police try to electrocute the blob. This fails, but Steve figures out that CO_2 fire extinguishers will freeze it. With the help of the teenagers, the fire department freezes the blob, and the air force flies it to the Arctic.

As is the situation of the teens in *The Giant Gila Monster*, these teens are at first harassed by authority figures and not believed by them. While the police force is distrustful of the teens, one policeman, Jim, shows outright contempt for them, though Dave, the police chief, shows sympathy. When Steve shows Jim and Dave the doctor's office, Jim accuses Steve and his other teenage friends of having engineered the chaos of the room as a stunt. Dave reserves judgment, but decides to send Jane and Steve home and calls Jane's and Steve's parents to fetch them. Jane's father, who is the high school principal, displays his selfishness when he asks Jane, "Don't you realize what this could do to me?" Like Wheeler in *The Giant Gila Monster*, Jane's father shows concern only for his reputation, but no concern at all for the welfare of Jane or the other teenagers. This is especially ironic since his job calls for him to oversee and protect young people at the high school. Even though

Steve's father is not abrasive, he does not believe Steve's story about a monster. No one does. So, Steve and the other teenagers must band together in order to save the town from the alien threat.

Interestingly, *The Blob* shows the teenagers saving the day by engaging in what was perceived in fifties society as the behavior of juvenile delinquents. Both Steve and Jane sneak out of their homes in the middle of the night. They collect up the other teenagers, who are watching a midnight horror film called *Daughter of Horror,* and they proceed, first, to try and warn people. Still, no one believes them. A necking couple, a bartender, and a drunken man at a party all laugh at the teenagers' attempts to save them. When Steve and Jane find the blob in his father's grocery store, they call the police station, but Jim rejects their plea, selfishly indulging in paranoiac fantasy: "I think they've got it in for me," he says, citing his war record as the motivation for the teens' hatred of him. After having their efforts rejected by the police, the teens turn to more extreme means of alerting people to the threat. Steve tells them, "We tried to do it the right way. Now, we're going to wake this town up ourselves." The teens blow their car horns, set off civil-defense sirens, and call the fire department. The crowd won't listen to Steve even then. One man says, "If we're in trouble, where are the police?" Finally, Dave, the police chief, is convinced and agrees to help Steve and the other teens find the blob.

The true virtue of the teenagers in *The Blob* lies in their ability to act quickly. Even though Dave is sympathetic to Steve, he wants to leave any further investigation until the next day. When the police station starts to get calls reporting strange occurrences in the town, Dave comments, "I guess there's nothing here that won't wait until morning." Even once everyone has been forced to accept the existence of the blob, it is the teenagers who act quickly, taking Principal Martin to the high school to get the needed fire extinguishers to freeze the blob. Ironically, Martin must grab a rock and break the glass of the school door in order to get in, again referencing how the film refigures delinquent behavior as a positive force in the midst of a crisis. Adult authorities fail in both *The Giant Gila Monster* and *The Blob* because of their caution and lack of open-mindedness, but the horror itself remains safely distant in a reptilian freak and an alien substance. Other teen-centered horror films from the decade, however, locate horror within adult culture itself.

I Was a Teenage Werewolf tells the story of a troubled teen, Tony, who cannot control his temper. Although a model student, he is continually in trouble due to constant fights he provokes with other teenagers. A police detective, Donovan, recommends Tony to a psychologist, Dr. Alfred Brandon. Brandon, however, has no desire to help Tony, but, rather, begins to use him as a guinea pig, utilizing a substance he has invented called scopolomene, which causes humans to revert to primitive forms. Tony transforms into a werewolf. On two separate occasions, he kills one of of his classmates, with the result that he becomes a fugitive from justice. He returns to Brandon's lab, confronts Brandon, and kills him, after which a policeman, ordered to do so by Detective Donovan, kills Tony.

Initially in the film, we see Tony as the embodiment of the psychopathic teenage delinquent. In the opening sequence, he fights with a friend, relentlessly attacking him, and finally picking up a shovel to hit him with. The police have to break up the fight. But Tony is more than a troubled teen: he is one whose behavior verges on the criminally psychopathic. Lindner comments on teenage psychopaths that they "invariably show a naive inability to understand or appreciate that other individuals as well have rights: they are also inaccessible and intolerant of the demands and pleas of the community, scornful of communal enterprise and spirit, suspicious of the motives of community-minded people" (8). The film sets up Tony's character as a case study of a Lindner psychopath.[4] When Tony's girlfriend's parents suggest that he get a job, he scorns their suggestion, pointing to a local bank teller who stole money and disappeared, subsequently gambling it away. He shows a complete lack of concern for other people, telling Detective Brandon, "People bug me!" He routinely subjects his girlfriend, Arlene, and his father to verbal abuse. Yet, the film does not hold Tony completely responsible for his actions. Tony tells Arlene: "I say things. I do things. I don't know why."

When Detective Donovan suggests that Tony visit a psychologist, Brandon, the film adopts the position that juvenile delinquency is a disease. This is typical of fifties commentaries on the social problems of teenagers and also illustrates how this social issue was one conducive to representation in the horror genre. Joseph Reed has argued that the concept of disease is central to the horror film: "Horror is, in fact, several different diseases: each kind of movie embodies, enacts, comes to confront something like a disease . . . Each subgenre has fantastic trapping and results and an intensely empathetic outline and form, so we are alienated and attracted, somewhat as we are by someone who is ill" (76). If horror plays on the audience's attraction/repulsion for disease, postwar audiences would have been attuned to the sensational disease of juvenile delinquency. Fine, for example, argues that delinquency, like a physical disease, can be cured: "Just as we are pressing ahead to find the causes and cures for polio, cancer, and multiple sclerosis, so we must press forward to eliminate the causes of juvenile delinquency" (116). In Lindner's pre-war study of delinquency, *Rebel without a Cause*, he identified the problem as assuming "More and more the proportions of a plague" (15-16). By the time of a 1954 interview, Lindner saw the youth of America as "literally sick with an aberrant condition of mind formerly confined to a few distressed souls but now epidemic over the earth" (qtd. in Oakley 270). The film makes a mild attempt to trace some of Tony's problems to his home life: his father is weak and his mother is dead. When Tony's father learns of Tony's transformation and of the murders he has committed, he blames himself: "Maybe I should've remarried," he tells a reporter. Still, the primary focus is on the inexplicable disease of juvenile delinquency that afflicts Tony. Yet, the complication of the film, and something that makes it a teen-focused horror film and not a melodrama, is that the cure is worse than the disease.

In the film, Tony's suspicion of authority, which is ostensibly part of the disease he is suffering from, is borne out as a correct one: when he trusts Dr. Brandon, he literally becomes a monster. Thus, while the film explores juvenile delinquency as a social problem, it also affirms teenagers' fear of authority by displaying the horror genre's deep-seated suspicions regarding the medical establishment. Thus, the mad scientist of sf/horror assumes the structural position of the corrupt authority figure that troubled teens. As a contrast to *I Was a Teenage Werewolf*, a mainstream melodrama like *Rebel without a Cause* shows intense sympathy for the teen characters—Jim, Judy, and Plato—but it does not question adult authority, per se. The teens in this film want to be adults. The worst that the adult world can be accused of in that film is of being weak, as, for example, Jim's father is.[5] In *I Was a Teenage Werewolf*, adult authority is ultimately even more psychotic than the diseased juvenile culture it presumes to treat.[6]

Dr. Brandon is a mad scientist of the atomic age. As the consulting psychologist at an aircraft plant, he has on his side the authority of science, medicine, and the corporation. Detective Donovan perceives him to be a philanthropist because he treats troubled teens free of charge, but the reality is that he views human life as no different from that of a guinea pig, as he makes clear to his conscience-stricken assistant, Hugo Wagner. Brandon's scientific experiments are based on the premise that human society is moving toward self-destruction. Brandon tells Hugh that "mankind is on the verge of self-destruction." His solution to this problem is to "unleash the savage instincts" and allow mankind to start over again.

Brandon's malaise is typical of those postwar thinkers who believed that the world was self-destructing. Nuclear war, communism, anti-communism, conformism and other ills were put forth as signs of the imminent breakdown of society. Juvenile delinquency was yet another of these symptoms. Fine, for example, laments the decline of American society, holding up Okinawan culture as more sane than American culture: "When you compare it with our western world—where every two minutes a man, woman, or child enters a mental hospital for observation or care, where half our hospital beds are occupied by the mentally diseased, where more than half the ills in the doctor's office are psychosomatic—Okinawa makes you wonder" (55). A perception of society on the verge of destruction paradoxically motivates both Tony's psychosis and Brandon's insane medical experiments. Both men have a deep-seated hatred for society. When Detective Donovan tells Tony he has to learn to adjust, he angrily replies, "Adjust to what?" Brandon might give the same reply, since he believes that humans are better off living through their animal instincts and evolving all over again in order to create a less self-destructive society.

I Was a Teenage Werewolf locates the horror of juvenile delinquency in a very specific area of authority: the scientific community. This film associates the horrors of science that shaped the period—the A-bomb, then the H-bomb, both leading to impending nuclear war—with the problem of psychotic teens. Fine is tentative in associating delinquency with fear of nuclear holocaust, commenting "that we are living in times of great tension and rapid change goes without saying. What effect the threat of atomic war may have upon the increasing incidence of delinquency, we do not know" (109). However, later studies have made connections between the angst of fifties teens and the potential doom of nuclear war that hung over their heads. In his study of nuclear culture, Spencer Weart notes that "a psychological survey of young people in the mid-1960s confirmed that in their thoughts of imminent nuclear bombing, reality was reinforcing adolescent fantasies about inadequate and destructive adults" (340). If authority figures had not only failed to provide teenagers adequate role models, but had, insanely, created a weapon capable of destroying the world, then who could be surprised that teenage culture was in degeneration?

Postwar commentator Lewis Mumford feared that the suspicion pervading American society would result in decadence: "We can posit the familiar forms of these regressive reactions: escape in fantasy would be one: purposeless sexual promiscuity would be another: narcotic indulgence would be a third" (*Sanity* 30). Mumford's view of a degenerated American state, devoid of reason and living for the moment, is the one posited by Brandon, and the one unconsciously perceived by Tony.

Ultimately, *I Was a Teenage Werewolf* presents a very harsh view of the problem of authority and juvenile delinquency. As Tony and Brandon destroy each other there seems to be little hope for a solution to the problem presented. All Detective Donavon can do to help Tony at the end of the film is to kill him. Thus, the horror genre comes to a much more hopeless conclusion about the problem of juvenile delinquency than do mainstream films such as *Rebel without a Cause* or *The Unguarded Moment*. In each of these films, the audience is left with hope for a cure to the delinquency problem.

Ultimately, *The Giant Gila Monster*, *The Blob*, and *I Was a Teenage Werewolf* convey images of a world where authority is deeply flawed and frequently monstrous. Moreover, these films suggest that in order to negotiate the dangerous world they live in teens must either steer clear of authority figures or assume authority themselves. The teens cannot rely on teachers, doctors, scientists, policemen, or parents. Fifties horror films project the postwar irony that the drive toward self-destruction embodied in the creation of nuclear weapons is frequently cloaked in the language of self-preservation. For instance, in order to better mankind, Tony must be made into a werewolf. These films provide a glimpse into the insanity at the heart of many fifties authority figures, an insanity that, at least as far as teen-focused horror films are concerned, was much more terrifying than juvenile delinquency could ever be.

The deep-seated suspicion of male authority asserted in teen-themed horror films was matched by another sub-genre of fifties horror that located social problems within the realm of feminine influence.

ASTOUNDING SHE-MONSTERS:
FEMININITY IN FIFTIES HORROR FILMS

The association of femininity with a destructive force is common-place in the Western tradition. The horror genre particularly has drawn on the feminine's capacity to encode the monstrous and the destructive from Bram Stoker's monstrous vampire women in *Dracula* to more recent incarnations of the destructive feminine in horror films such as *The Exorcist, The Brood,* and the *Alien* films.[1] Fifties America was particularly haunted by the notion of the destructive feminine. While a common stereotype of that culture is one in which the feminine is non-threatening, such as in popular sit-coms of the period like *I Love Lucy* and *Father Knows Best,* in both fiction and nonfiction, another image of the feminine came to bear on American society. Sociologists such as Philip Wylie and Edward Strecker promoted an image of a dangerous, degenerate, and potentially subversive form of femininity that went by the term Momism. Discussions of Momism sought to instill in the reader a fear of a degenerative femininity, one which was present in contemporary society, but which partook of the mythological. In *Generation of Vipers,* for example, Wylie associates Mom with evil mythological women: "I give you Medusa and Stheno and Euyale. I give you the harpies and the witches, and the Fates . . . I give you Proserpine, the Queen of Hell. The five-and-ten-cent store Lilith, the mother of Cain, the black widow who is poisonous and eats her mate" (216). While critics have noted that the femmes fatales who dominated forties American films diminished in number in fifties films, the horror genre continued to engage the issue of the dangerous feminine within the specifics of contemporary debates over what women's proper position should be in fifties America.[2] *House of Wax, Phantom of the Rue Morgue, The Astounding She-Monster,* and "Morella" all emphasize the dangers of a parasitic femininity that threatens not only men but the entire social fabric as well.

Among the competing discourses that sought to define femininity in the postwar era, one of the most visible and controversial, as we have seen, was Momism. Wylie's popular and influential 1942 book *Generation of Vipers,* which the author updated for a 1955 edition, introduced momism into the American mainstream. As Jennifer Terry notes, "'mom'-bashing gained industrial strength during the decade following World War II, as bad mothers became powerful career vehicles for a host of sexist columnists, legislators, movie directors, and most notably, psychiatrists who heaped upon mothers culpability for everything from juvenile delinquency to totalitarianism" (169). Wylie's melodramatic writing style and outrageous accusations made his account of the degenerative influence of femininity on society notoriously well known. Wylie's argument is that American mothers have created a cult of worship of femininity that is progressively degenerating American men and the society in general.

Wylie argues that for several reasons Momism is a recent problem. One cause is the increase in laborsaving devices that allows women to have a good deal of free time and longer life spans: "Usually, until very recently, mom folded up and died of hard work somewhere in middle age" (199). Because women are not dying in middle age, and because they do not have to engage in hard manual labor, they are free to mount a propaganda campaign for irrationality manifested in soap operas, women's magazines, and other outlets that promote the Cinderella fantasy. Wylie compares these women to Hitler and Goebbels and blames Momism for World War II. In his additions to the 1955 version, he blames women for McCarthyism and the cold war: "'McCarthyism,' the rule of unreason is at one with momism: a noble end aborted by sickminded means, a righteous intent—in terrorism fouled and tyranny foundered" (196). For Wylie, Momism is a disease that is leading American men and American society to self-destruction. Wylie sees Mom lurking everywhere, especially beneath the surface of all women, maintaining that "she is the bride at every funeral and the corpse at every wedding" (198). Death images are particularly evident in Wylie's writing. Momism is wrapping American men in "a shroud" (196). Wylie concludes his essay dramatically by stating, "I give you mom. I give you the destroying mother. I give you her justice—from which have never removed the eye bandage. I give you the angel. And point to the sword in her hand. I give you death—the hundred million deaths" (215-16). Far from belittling women as insignificant and meaningless, Wylie elevates them to mythological heights, as possessing the ability to bring destruction to an entire civilization.

The discourse of Momism taps into cultural associations between the feminine and death, ones that the horror film typically addresses. In *Over Her Dead Body: Death, Femininity, and the Aesthetic*, Elisabeth Bronfen explores Western culture's association of the feminine with death. Western art's fascination with the figure of the dead woman, or woman as bringer of death, argues Bronfen, is the result on the part of male artists to deny their own mortality. By allowing the feminine to stand for death, men can disavow their own mortality and weakness. Yet the feminine death figure functions as an uncanny one. With her sexual difference she allows the man to disavow his own death, while simultaneously reminding him of death through her similarity to him. Bronfen believes that the feminine body as embodiment and carrier of death is a figure for the lost maternal body: "What repeatedly returns in ever the same guise, or what the subject seeks to return to, is the facticity beneath and beyond images and symbols—death, as originary loss of the maternal body, of a full unity" (325). Momism renders particularly transparent these machinations, since the object of the attack is the maternal feminine, the destructive mother who is hiding beneath the exteriors of young, beautiful women. Wylie comments that "Mom steals from the generation of women behind her," taking their husband's love and possessing them for their ultimate transformation into Mom (208).[3]

Bataille's ideas regarding the loss of autonomy in the realm of the erotic relate to anxieties regarding the feminine. While Wylie paints a portrait of an all-consuming mom who seeks to transform the culture, Bataille's view of the feminine, with regard to the male lover, is also one of fear and loss of identity. Bataille comments, for example, that "for the man in lover . . . the fervour of love may be felt more violently than physical desire is . . . Eroticism as seen by the objective intelligence is something monstrous" (*Erotism* 19; 37). Thus, from Bataille's perspective, the creation of a monstrous feminine is merely a way of bodying forth the monstrousness of eroticism itself. Thereby the object of masculine desire, the feminine, takes on monstrous and engulfing qualities. Horror films, with their obsessions with death and loss, are particularly suited to convey an idea of the feminine as bearer of death and corruption.

House of Wax (1953) tells the story of sculptor Henry Jarrod, an idealist who creates wax figures for artistic purposes but becomes bitter and murderous after his partner, Matthew Burke, burns down their wax museum for insurance money, an act that results in Jarrod becoming horribly disfigured in the fire. Jarrod begins killing people and pouring wax over their bodies, then displaying them in his new museum. Sue Allen recognizes a friend of hers, Cathy Gray, who has been murdered by Jarrod in order to serve as his Joan of Arc. With the help of the police and her sculptor boyfriend, Scott Andrews, Sue uncovers Jarrod's sinister plan. Sue herself is almost made into a wax figure by Jarrod, but Andrews and the police save her, and Jarrod dies after falling into a vat of wax.

Jarrod's desire to create feminine perfection in his wax figures contrasts with the women we see in the film, some of whom display the telltale signs of Momism. Jarrod idealizes the female figures he has created, believing that they are the epitome of feminine perfection. At the beginning of the film, before his first museum burns down, Jarrod takes pride in his Marie Antoinette, even lovingly holding her hand and speaking to her in the presence of a man who is interested in buying the museum. Jarrod takes the figure's hand, looks lovingly into her eyes, and says, "Forgive me, my dear, for disclosing your intimate secrets." Jarrod's greatest desire is that the world appreciate Marie's beauty. When Matthew sets the museum on fire, he chooses to start the conflagration by setting fire to the Marie figure's skirt, thereby indicating that he knows how much she means to Jarrod. Jarrod's attempt to create feminine perfection in the form of wax figures leads him to murder women in order to transform them into flawless images of feminine beauty.

The transformation of Cathy Gray, Sue's best friend and Matthew's fiancée, best illustrates how Jarrod takes the feminine of Momism and translates it into his ideal of femininity. Even though the film is set in the nineteenth century, Cathy's lifestyle and attitudes are redolent of Wylie's idea of degenerative femininity. Cathy is a kept woman whose only concern is going out and getting as much money as she can. She is proud that Matthew is interested in her, because it means she can rise socially. As Matthew tells Cathy about the fire at the museum, she feigns interest, but is only trying to find out about the insurance money. When Matthew tells her the amount he is getting from the museum, Cathy immediately demands marriage. Wylie portrays Mom in her youth as a "pretty girl" who "blindfolded her man" and then, "finally, having him sightless and whirling, she snitched his checkbook" (200). Cathy shows no sadness over Matthew's death, as she immediately begins unwittingly going out with a disguised Jarrod. He finally kills Cathy by slipping poison to her in a drink. Sue has previously called attention to Cathy's heavy drinking, another sign that links her with the degenerative feminine of Momism. Wylie's mom is a heavy drinker: "She drinks moderately, which is to say, two or three cocktails before dinner every night and a brandy and a couple of highballs afterward. She doesn't count the two cocktails she takes before lunch" (202). When Jarrod steals Cathy's body from the morgue, two orderlies witness the corpse of a female suicide victim sit up due to the effects of embalming fluid. One of the orderlies comments, "Just like a woman. They always have to have the last word." When Jarrod transforms Cathy from social-climbing parasite into Joan of Arc, he has taken degenerative Momism and changed it into virginal self-sacrifice.

Images of degenerative femininity are present in the film in other ways as well. When Jarrod gives a guided tour of his new museum, the film emphasizes the women customers. One woman looks at Little Egypt belly dancing in a skimpy costume and tries to imitate it. Another woman peers into the bathtub to try to catch a fuller view of Marat's wax body. The women are sexually degenerate and also bloodthirsty as they thrill to the scenes of violence in the museum. Further, the images in the museum emphasize feminine danger and degeneracy. Anne Boleyn and Charlotte Corday indicate feminine transgression. The wax head severed by the guillotine is a woman's head. The figure being tortured on the rack by the Inquisition is also that of a woman. The women touring the museum revel in these images, but one woman faints when she sees the figure of a man known as the Modern Bluebeard. The idealistic Jarrod, who once wanted to create art, now creates sensation, and the film tells us that it is women who are lapping up these representations of violence and death. Wylie believed that popular culture was the arena in which Momism promoted "hidden cruelty, and the foreshadow of a national death" (215). Further Wylie maintained that because women "possess some eighty percent of the nation's money" they are the consumers who determine what entertainment will be available to all Americans. In Geoffrey Gorer's discussion of what he sees as the matriarchy of post-war America, he cites the fact that women dominate consumerism, making "more than three quarters of the retail purchases in the United States" (61). In a 1958 book by the editors of *Look* magazine entitled *The Decline of the American Male*, the woman as dominating consumer is also a common theme. The editors note that Walt Disney gears his films toward American women (19). As *House of Wax* indicates, women choose sensational violence as their entertainment of choice.

While the film portrays negative images of a degenerative and unscrupulous femininity, it counters that image with Sue Allen. Although Jarrod wants to transform Sue into Marie Antoinette, for her that would not be an elevation, as the transformation into Joan of Arc is for Cathy, but a lowering. Sue is not money-grubbing and lazy. She desperately seeks work, and loses out on a job as a hat check girl because she will not capitulate to the manager's sexual demands. She turns to Mrs. Andrews and her son Scott only when she is suspected by the police of being Cathy's killer. Further, Sue works hard to discover the truth about Cathy's death and eventually exposes Jarrod as a killer. As Joanne Meyerowitz notes, what was particularly demonized in fifties culture was the woman of leisure. Thus, misogynists like Wylie and *Ladies Home Journal* and other pro-women magazines met in their hatred of the parasitic woman. Meyerowitz notes that "The flip side of this emphasis on hard work was a condemnation of idleness and frivolity. Articles opposed meaningful work to activities coded as the trivial pursuits of the woman of leisure: bridge playing, aimless shopping, and 'summers on the Rivera'" (1461). Because Sue seeks to earn her living rather than being a kept woman and becomes involved with Scott because she is truly attracted to him, she represents an alternative to the other images of destructive femininity present in the film.

Another horror film also presents a series of images of dangerous and destructive femininity but also counters it with an image of the proper woman. *Phantom of the Rue Morgue* (1954) is a loose adaptation of Edgar Allan Poe's story "Murders in the Rue Morgue." The film focuses on a series of unexplained murders. All the victims are beautiful women. Professor Dupin, a scientist who teaches at a Paris University, is falsely accused of the murders. Eventually, Dr. Marais, a behaviorist, is revealed to be the murderer. He has used a gorilla to kill his girlfriends, all of whom have disappointed him because they failed to live up to the memory of his dead wife. Jeanette, Dupin's fiancée almost becomes Marais' last victim, but is saved by Dupin. The gorilla murders Marais after being chased up a tree by the police and Dupin.

The women who are Marais' victims illustrate a view of women as sexually alluring, yet dangerous. The first victim, Yvonne, is a knife-thrower's assistant. The film portrays her as a fickle, sexually promiscuous woman who collects students as lovers. The knife thrower, René, is jealous of her other lovers and almost injures her during their stage act. While watching the act Jeanette comments, "Look at his face. He really wants to hurt her." Before the gorilla mutilates Yvonne, we see her looking at a collection of photographs of her lovers. She undresses, revealing sexy underwear, then the murder occurs. Yvonne's sexual allure is hence implicated in the violent murder that befalls her. Her allure combined with her faithlessness has caused Marais to unleash the gorilla on her and ruin her beauty in a most violent manner. Thus, the cruelty at the base of eroticism that Bataille discerns expresses itself in the violent murder (*Eroticism* 90). After her murder, René is a suspect and one woman reports to Inspector Bonnard that she has overheard Yvonne telling René, "You've mauled me enough for one night." While Yvonne represents the dangers of feminine promiscuity, Marais' next victim, Arlette, illustrates a woman who uses her sexual allure for financial gain.

Arlette, an artist's model, poses nude for an artist, but slaps his face when he makes an advance, asking, "When do I get paid?" When the artist refuses her money because of the expensive bracelet that she wears, a gift from Marais, Arlette attempts to destroy the portrait she has been modeling for. The artist tells her, "No painting, no pay," and she puts the knife down that she has been threatening the painting with. The gorilla then crashes through the window, splattering red paint all over the portrait. Arlette's sexual allure, combined with her hardened desire for money, has resulted in her becoming a victim of Marais' beast.

In a scene that follows close upon Arlette's murder, we see Marais lecturing to a class about the killer instinct in a woman who is now a deaf mute. He says that the woman, Marie, wanted to kill her husband for leaving her, describing her as "a vampire, preying on man." Because she has been torn between instinct and the demands of civilization, she has retreated into a world of her own. The film emphasizes to us the dangers of women's passions, finally revealing that Marais' homicidal nature has developed because his wife has rejected him by killing herself.

After framing Dupin, Marais begins to court Jeanette, finally showing her his private rooms at his zoo and the gorilla he keeps hidden from everyone but his assistant and accomplice, Jacques. Staring at the portrait of his wife, Marais tells Jeanette that after his wife's death he has been motivated by a "desperate wish to understand the human mind." After showing Jeanette the gorilla, Marais attempts to kiss her, but she rejects him, telling him, "Your voice. The touch of your hand. They're frightening." Jeanette then tells him that his wife killed herself because she was afraid of him. Marais becomes angered and tells Jeanette that all women are the same, saying that after his wife's death, "I wanted to kill all others like her." Thus, the horrible murders are the product of women's unfaithfulness, the result of a sexual allure combined with a hard-heartedness. The film spares Jeanette because she is virtuous, yet she also mocks Marais and provokes his murderous anger. Because the gorilla recognizes her goodness and refuses to kill her, the force of Marais is stopped, and Jeanette is free to marry Dupin at the end of the film as he gives her a bracelet similar to the ones Marais has given his victims.

While *House of Wax* and *Phantom of the Rue Morgue* illustrate that proper femininity can stop degenerative processes in society, another fifties horror film suggests that American femininity has so degenerated that it calls forth an alien monster, its outer-space doppelgänger. *The Astounding She-Monster* (1958) is a low-budget film that focuses on a geologist who sights a meteor falling from the sky. Two criminals and their moll take refuge in his cabin along with their kidnap victim, a socialite, when a she-monster from outer space causes them to wreck their car. The she-monster pursues them, killing everyone except the geologist and the socialite, who devise a way to destroy her. After her destruction they find a message from her planet that relates that she is a peaceful emissary sent to ask Earth to join a federation of planets rather than continue in its course toward self-destruction.

The dissipated woman of leisure seen in the character of Cathy in *House of Wax* is central to *The Astounding She-Monster's* portrayal of monstrous femininity. The film opens with a warning from the narrator that the destruction of earth is imminent: "Are we today on the point of repeating this cosmic suicide?" he asks, referring to other planets that have self-destructed due to nuclear weapons. The film then immediately switches to a focus on the socialite, Margaret. It makes an associative link between destruction of the earth and the leisured woman. The narrator sarcastically relates that Margaret is beset by problems: "Overslept. Late for cocktails." He implies that her kidnapping is justified. Through her useless, leisured life she has invited the kidnappers. Further, the narrator implies that Margaret has called forth the she-monster by stressing that it is her fate to meet the creature. The film thus associates Margaret with the self-destruction of the arms race that forces an alien culture to intervene to try to stop it, an association that seems strange, but one made by Wylie as well. In his 1955 revisions to *Generation of Vipers*, he associates the arms race with Momism: "The enemy explodes uranium, plutonium, hydrogen; still they absurdly cry: 'Keep these things forever an American secret. A great victory for momish thinking" (217). Other images of femininity reinforce this view of American women facilitating the earth's destruction.

When the criminals arrive at the geologist's house, much emphasis is placed on the moll, a middle-aged blonde who drinks excessively. As they drive away with Margaret in tow, the moll finishes an entire bottle of hard liquor and then tosses the bottle out the window. When she gets to the cabin, the first thing she says is, "You got a drink in this dump?" When the geologist gives her a bottle, she drinks directly out of it. One of the criminals tells the geologist that the moll used to be a society woman. He met her when she was passed out in an alley. Her drunkenness exemplifies the dissipation of the American woman as Wylie saw it, and also emphasizes the danger of such dissipation. When the criminal asks her to guard the geologist and the socialite, she shows herself to be a security risk. Her desire for more and more alcohol makes her unable to guard them. Her weakness highlights a central fear associated with momism: the idea that the 1950s woman was susceptible to and made those around her susceptible to foreign takeover. Terry argues that in the discourse of Momism, a woman was "the agent of internal decay, browbeating her children and husband, succumbing, in bitterness to agoraphobia, or worse feminism and communism" (185). In their 1956 book, *Their Mothers' Daughters*, in which they attempt to define what true femininity is,

Strecker and Lathbury warn that women must be strong, because the entire future of democracy is at stake. They advocate the adoption of real femininity because "we would know that our democratic stature, strength, and security would be immeasurably increased. The children of these women would not be deceived by the economic, social, political, and ideological false prophets of the day" (35). In America, woman's weakness had specific connotations: a weak and dissipated woman was a security risk that threatened the very fabric of American life. Margaret and the moll, with their dissipated and useless lifestyles call forth the she-monster, who also serves as a figure for destructive femininity.

The she-monster is a figure of sexual allure. In the original trailer for the film, the narrator describes her as "a woman so intriguing that the face and figure fascinate." When the she-monster first appears on the screen, the narrator says "evil unto evil." She frightens the animals in the forest with her unnaturalness. A snake approaches her, and she kills it. When she causes the criminals' car wreck, one of the men says that he was distracted by "a naked dame." The she-monster is an Eve figure who uses sexual allure to draw in her victims and kill them. She represents the mythological power that Wylie associates with the postwar American woman. Wylie discusses the American woman as a Gorgon who reveals her monstrous side only after she has snared a man into marriage, resulting in American men being turned "not to stone, but to slime" (208). Thus, while the rather tacked-on ending of the film associates the she-monster with a peaceful planetary force, her real allure is her danger. As the double of the moll and Margaret, she illustrates the destruction that will result from their type of femininity.

Curiously, though, the film spares Margaret's life. While the moll and the criminals are killed by the she-monster, Margaret and the geologist escape. Much like that of Sue in *House of Wax*, it is Margaret's ability to engage in useful work that saves her. Because she is, oddly enough, informed about scientific matters—"Isn't radium in a solid form a metal?" she asks the geologist—she can work productively with the geologist to stop the threat of the she-monster. As in *House of Wax*, in *The Astounding She-Monster* the objects of intense scorn are idle women, Wylie's parasitic women who feed off men and off American society.

Another example of the parasitic but powerful woman is at the center of "Morella." "Morella" is an episode in Roger Corman's *Tales of Terror* (1962), a collection of three short films based loosely on the work of Edgar Allan Poe. In "Morella," Lenora Locke returns home after having been banished from her parents' house. She finds her father, Locke, living as an alcoholic in a ruined mansion. He has preserved the body of his dead wife, Morella, in her bed. He rejects Lenora because prior to her sudden death a few months after Lenora's birth, Morella blamed the child for her own impending death. Locke has refused to see Lenora. She has returned home because she is dying at the age of twenty-six. Locke eventually forgives Lenora, and this forgiveness results in Morella's spirit returning and possessing the body of Lenora after first killing her. Finally, Morella strangles Locke to death out of revenge in a climatic scene in which the mansion burns down.[4]

"Morella" presents us with a feminine force so strong and powerful that it continues to exert control over people's lives even after death. Morella is a destructive force that ruins her husband's and daughter's lives from the grave. In his discussion of "Mother-Land," his name for the United States, Gorer notes that the American woman is frequently perceived as parasitic because of her strong influence over children both as mother and as teacher: "This picture of the clinging mother, and the fear of such vampirelike possession—the hidden fear that one may one-self have been so possessed—is one of the components in the very strong ambivalence American men feel toward women" (64). Locke's dependence upon Morella is childlike. Locke seems almost to have been possessed by Morella while she was alive. He tells Lenora that when she died "I died with her." He says that after losing her he became "a walking corpse" because "she was my life." Morella's influence on Locke has been a degenerative one, making him into a reclusive alcoholic who has rejected his own daughter.

Morella is a woman of leisure who spreads her dissipation both to her husband and her child. Locke relates that Morella perished because she was adamant about giving a party too soon after Lenora's birth. Locke says, "she had to dress up in her finest gown, dance, sing." When she collapses at the party, she blames Lenora for her imminent death, "It was the baby," she repeats again and again to Locke. Morella has not only ruined Locke's life by transmitting her degenerative influence to him by making him dependent on her, but she ruins Lenora's life as well.

One fear that informs momism discourse is the notion that the feminine influence of the mother is not only harming boys, but also girls. Lenora tells Locke that she is divorced, but it hasn't surprised her because "I'd failed in my relationships with men, many times, many times." Strecker and Lathbury condemn the mother who out of a sense of jealousy destroys her daughter's chances for sexual fulfillment. They comment that "We have a few more remarks to make about the most dangerous of moms, the one who tries to destroy her daughter's future sexual happiness. This mother performs an emotional abortion upon her own child. We could almost wish that such an operation would be declared criminal and made punishable by law" (140). Morella has destroyed Lenora's chances for a happy marriage by accusing her of causing her death. Further, in the film Morella's spirit comes forth at the very moment that Locke and Lenora reconcile and Locke embraces his daughter. Morella's appearance at this point suggests that Morella suffers from sexual jealousy with regard to Lenora. The possession of the daughter by the mother that informs momism is literalized in "Morella," as Morella takes over her daughter's body and kills her in the process of doing so.

Perhaps Morella embodies the monstrous feminine for fifties/early sixties American society most of all because she rejects outright the role of mother. If momism condemns the grasping mother, it condemns even more strongly the mother who is perceived to be unnatural, the one who rejects her child, and, thus, by implication, rejects her biological womanhood. Strecker and Lathbury advise: "The main function of women is to give birth to children and 'make' a home in which they may be reared" (29). Morella's rejection of the role of the motherhood taken to the grotesque extreme of blaming her child for her own death makes her a monstrous figure. As we discover at the end of the film, her anger is not directed just at Lenora, but at Locke as well, whom she also blames for her death. After she has killed Lenora and Locke, Morella's spirit returns to her body, and the corpse smiles. Morella is satisfied that she has gotten her revenge on both husband and child.

The creation of a mythological feminine in the concept of Momism combined specific postwar fears of leisure with a more universal fear of the feminine as dangerous. Generalized fear of social degeneration as the result of the growing leisure society and the escalating cold war was typical of the American 1950s. In a world in which the economic prosperity of the middle class made many fear degeneration within the United States, the leisured woman came to embody this particular horror. Fictional females in horror films such as Cathy, the woman of *Rue Morgue*, the she-monster, and Morella spoke to a conjoining in 1950s horror films between an ancient western suspicion of the dangerous, castrating feminine and a specific fear of the leisured woman who was causing the ruin of postwar America.

CONCLUSION

Horror films provide a guide to many of the sociological fears of the cold war era. Because of their frequently naive approach to the fears of the time, they give the audience vivid metaphors for the monsters that plagued British and American society in the 1950s-1960s. Bataille argues that in human society, "Violence, and death signifying violence, have a double meaning. On the one hand the horror of death drives us off, for we prefer life; on the other an element at once solemn and terrifying fascinates us and disturbs us profoundly" (*Erotism* 45). The violence, death, and eroticism at the core of the horror genre may appeal to us on a universal level because it allows a space for us to contemplate death. In a famous statement on horror, Stephen King has argued that when reading or viewing a work of horror, "We're afraid of the body under the sheet. It's our body. And the great appeal of horror fiction through the ages is that it serves as a rehearsal for our own deaths" (xvi). While the fascination with death, and with our own mortality especially, characterizes horror fiction in a universal way, a specific fascination with death haunted the cold war era.

In an age when warning audiences of impending death was the order of the day for popular non-fiction, horror films allowed an area where this fear of death could be lived out to its horrible conclusion. In a time when newspapers articles, such as one that appeared in the *St. Louis Post-Dispatch,* could declare that "science has signed the mammalian world's death warrant and deeded an earth in ruin to the ants" ("Decision"), horror films that could show giant men, werewolves, cowboy vampires, and alien children threatening the future of the planet seem very much in tune with the apocalyptic fears of the age.

In a time period in which enemies and potential situations of horror lurked everywhere, within the home, within the government, within the family, within the very self, horror films could speak adequately to the invasive fears of the cold war era. Thus whether we see the family invaded by a criminal or alien force such as in *The Bad Seed* and *Village of the Damned* or the very self threatened by take-over from something alien, such as in *Invasion of the Body Snatchers* and *Monster on the Campus,* these films chart cold war fears that there is no place to hide from communist infiltration, from the atomic bomb, from the forces of dehumanization that characterized post-World War II society. Monsters and potential monsters were lurking everywhere within cold war American and British imaginations. Horror films gave audiences a visual manifestation of their deepest fears.

NOTES

Introduction

1. See Mikita Brottman for an interesting discussion of *The Tingler* that combines psychoanalytic theory with a discussion of Castle's use of experimental audience-participation techniques.

2. For solid discussions of eroticism and horror, see Barbara Creed, *The Monstrous-Feminine: Film, Feminism, Psychoanalysis*, and David. J. Hogan *Dark Romance: Sexuality in the Horror Film.*

Chapter 1

1. While Siegel's film is clearly an example of science fiction, it also fits into the horror category because of its embracing of the irrational. Jack P. Rawlings argues that in fantasy (a category he places horror in) "cuts us off from the instinctive wisdom of the irrational. In science fiction, reason liberates us from the narrowness of our humanity. So fantasy and science fiction, inseparable companions though they may be, are more than different—they are natural enemies" (165). While I don't necessarily agree with so neat a division, Siegel's film clearly embraces the irrational over the reasonable. One of the central tenets of pejorative criticism of 1950s sf films has centered on the idea that, unlike 1950s sf books and stories, these films had too close a connection to horror. Richard Hodgens, for example, laments 1950s sf films' embracing of the monster motif, which, he believes, results in associating "science, the future, the different, and the unknown with nothing but irrational fear" (261).

2. For example, see Glen M. Johnson, who catalogues how the alien invasion becomes an overdetermined site for 1950s anxieties. Stuart Samuels explores 1950s fears of conformism expressed in the film. Le Gacy and Peter Biskind explore the fear of communism that circulates throughout the film. Hendershot ("Invaded Body") explores the connection between the film and fear of radiation contamination.

3. For discussions of sexuality in the film, see Nancy Steffen-Fluhr, Thomas B. Bryers, David Seed, and Hendershot ("One-Sex Body").

4. See David Seed for a more comprehensive analysis of the erotic in Finney's novel. Seed argues that Miles' rescue of Becky is described in sexual language and is a simulation of intercourse: "After the sexual rhythm of running to her house he enters her home by breaking a basement window, suggestive of guilt and also of bodily entry" (155).

5. The frame of *Invasion of the Body Snatchers* in which Miles is mistaken for a an insane man is an imposition of the studio's and not part of Siegel's original plan.

6. Judith Surkis argues that Bataille's model of eroticism presupposes a female subject who has already dissolved into the world of continuity: "The feminine dissolution is thus necessarily prior to the masculine, with his experience of continuity predicated on her prior and total self-loss" (20).

7. Robin Wood argues that because we never see Scottie get down from the gutter, "The effect is of having him, throughout the film, metaphorically suspended over a great abyss" (*Hitchcock* 111-12).

8. Ann West argues that *Vertigo* falls into Torodov's category of the fantastic because we can never resolve our uncertainty as to whether the ghost of Carlotta has a presence in the film or not. The inexplicable action of Judy at the end of the film makes us wonder "whether Judy/Madeleine really acted as a channel for the dead Carlotta after all. Is it especially strange, the audience must ask itself, that Judy/Madeleine should be confused and driven to her death by the emergence of a ghostly apparition?" (171).

9. For further discussion of the connection between Poe and Hitchcock, see Dennis R. Perry, who connects *Vertigo* to Poe's stories "The Fall of the House of Usher," "Ligeia," and "The Black Cat." See also DeLoy Simper, who connects Hitchcock's films to Poe's criticism.

10. Many critics have seen the film as revealing how man destroys woman through idealization in patriarchal culture. Tania Modelski sees Scottie's sadistic treatment of Judy as predicated on the fact that "like a woman, he was manipulated and used by Galvin Elster" (98). Wood makes a similar point, labeling Scottie's idealization as regression that denies "otherness and autonomy" ("Male" 228).

11. Some critics have viewed Midge as a positive center in the film. Deborah Linderman, for example, praises Midge's ability to de-fetishize woman (71). Others have seen the film rejecting what she embodies. Walter Poznar argues that Midge represents a shallow surface that would deny the "deeper realities of the human condition" (61).

12. Royal S. Brown makes the distinction between Midge designing underwear and Scottie desiring to be free of his corset. Using a Freudian framework, she associates this detail with Midge's superego function and Scottie's id desire. Madeleine/Judy wears no bra. As Louis Phillips notes, we see the absence of Madeleine's bra when we see her clothes hanging in Scottie's kitchen (188). The absence of the bra was actually a sop to the censors, but, paradoxically had the opposite effect: it further eroticized Madeleine (Aulier 100). In Truffaut's famous interview with Hitchcock, much is made of Kim Novak not wearing a bra in the Judy scenes (244).

13. Some critics have seen Scottie's idealization of Madeleine as foreclosing the possibility of sexual attraction. Katie Trumpener argues that Elster knows that Scottie "would rather desire a fiction (the unobtainable woman represented to him in art) than have a real woman to sleep with" (184).

14. Many critics have seen a process of Scottie identifying with Madeleine. Modelski argues that Scottie's fascination with Madeleine is caused by "her own fascination with death" (91). Wood argues that Scottie's attraction to Madeleine is a matter of "identification—the desire for annihilation" (*Hitchcock* 118). Elisabeth Bronfen has argued, using a Freudian/Lacanian model, that Scottie identifies "with precisely the position of nonexistence she [Madeleine] embodies" (119).

15. Donald O. Chankin sees this point of the film as the first time Judy/Madeleine and Scottie have made love (34).

16. Trumpener argues that the ending of Vertigo suggests that "Scottie's drama may repeat itself infinitely; he will 'never come to the end' of the mirrored corridor, he will always 'come back'" (186-87). Robin Wood believes that Scottie has been cured by Judy's death, but is left "empty, desolate" (*Hitchcock* 129). Bronfen suggests that the film leaves the question open as to whether Scottie has triumphed over death or been subjected to it (125). Brown believes that the last image of Scottie suggests that he has "defeated death through the quasi-ritualistic sacrifice of another human being" (34).

Chapter 2

1. William Paul makes a strong argument for considering *The Bad Seed* as a horror film. He argues that the film probably was not perceived as a horror film at the time because it was pioneering a new direction in horror: "*The Bad Seed* effectively brought horror home, domesticating it by locating what is most horrible *within* the family. If critics have not generally perceived it as a horror film, this is nonetheless its greatest importance for the horror genre in the 1970s and 1980s. Never before had middle-class homelife been the primary locus for horror; by the late 1970s it began to seem the only place" (270).

2. The novel and play versions end with Christine's death and Rhoda's survival. A friend reassures Kenneth that "at least Rhoda was spared. At least you have Rhoda to be thankful for" (217).

3. Paul notes that the film punishes both the transgressors: Christine, who must repent, and Rhoda, for whom "only total annihilation was good enough" (279).

4. Christopher Sharrett argues that the horror film's "heritage in the metaphysical" has caused it to turn to the supernatural to establish cause and effect (55). He maintains that by the early 1960s "a wrathful God" was replaced by an apocalypse brought about by "recognizable disintegration within the human community" (41). *The Bad Seed* clearly exists in a transition mode. While the

novel would locate apocalypse within human disintegration (even if biologically inherited), the film version represents a last gasp of a wrathful God. The critics' negative reactions to the ending indicate how metaphysical explanations for evil were on the wane even in the mid-1950s.

5. Further, the novel links Rhoda's behavior explicitly with the behavior of an animal. When Christine embraces her, we are told that she "submitted to the caress with that tolerant but withdrawn patience of the pet that can never quite be domesticated" (9). A psychiatrist at a school she attended previously concludes that "she was like a charming little animal that can never be trained to fit into the conventional patterns of existence . . ." (37; ellipsis in original).

6. Paul argues that the biological explanation provides a fantasy for an audience not wanting to deal with "a monster created by the nuclear family" (268). Williams argues that the biological explanation is a reaction against "liberal, environmentally based theories that were critical of social institutions" (87).

7. The novel describes Claude a "pale and remarkably thin, with a long, wedge-shaped face, and a full, pink underlip that puckered with an inappropriate sensousness" (19). Harry M Benshoff notes that the "sensitive young man" was a typical 1950s way of expressing the homosexual male. Frequently this type of young man was "doomed from the outset" (138). March's physical description links Claude with this type of young man. In the film Mrs. Breedlove suggests that Claude drowned because of his own weakness and fear. As Elaine Showalter discusses in her introduction to the novel March's own homosexuality is complexly encoded in the story of Rhoda. Showalter argues that "William March's mask concealed a man who felt that in his creative and sexual desires he himself was a bad seed" (xiii) is a reaction against "liberal, environmentally based theories that were critical of social institutions" (87).

8. Paul links Rhoda's crimes to concern about postwar consumerism. Rhoda's greed is thus "something that belongs to her culture" (274). Williams links Rhoda to McCarthy-era scapegoating. He also notes the connection between her actions and the Pentagon activities of her father, arguing that "it is more than coincidental that the film never discloses what Rhoda's father actually does" (88). Simmonds briefly links Rhoda's evil with "the wider context of national and international politics," but does not expand on this (300).

9. Paul notes that "When the daddies were away, the girls did play, but at the end, God, the ultimate patriarch, makes an appearance, and boy, is he angry!" (281).

10. See *The Human Radiation Experiments* for documentation of radiation experiments done by the military and the AEC on human subjects in the postwar era. See also Eileen Welsome's recent study of the experiments, *The Plutonium Files: America's Secret Medical Experiments in the Cold War*. She puts human faces on the victims.

11. Knee notes that in Helene's list of discoveries she omits nuclear weapons. Thus, "Andre's new machine would appear to stand in as a replacement for the atomic in both its continued mysteriousness and its ultimately mutating effect on Andre" (21).

12. Knee notes the link between the experiment and André and Hélène's marriage, concluding that André's transformation illustrates his "need to escape a heterosexual marriage," thus possibly coding him as homosexual (25).

13. Most critics feel sympathetic to Marion and her desires. Brill comments that "Marion wants to stop meeting in cheap hotels, to have family dinners on Sunday afternoons, to get married. Nothing more remarkable. Nothing less crucial" (228). Robin Wood argues that "It is Sam's fault that Marion steals the money, which has no importance to her" (143).

14. In the novel Mary is not motivated by erotic desire, but by a desire for respectability. She does not love Sam, but is concerned that she is past the marriageable age. Further, in the novel she does not sleep with Sam. As she admires her figure in the mirror she thinks, "She had a good figure. A *damned* good figure. Sam would like it" (50). Further, Mary makes calculated plans for stealing and escaping with the money. Her desire seems to be for financial acquisition and respectability and thus is not the transgressive desire of Marion in the film. Marion of the film would seem to contradict what Hitchcock found annoying about American woman: "Here they play at sex, like little girls playing house. I don't like women who have their sex hanging around their necks like jewelry and then if a man approaches them, they run away screaming for mother" (qtd. in Donohue).

15. Corber argues that Sam's "desire is clearly contingent upon meeting Marion secretly in cheap hotels" (211). Sam, thus, sees no problem with their relationship. What attracts him to the situation is its illicitness, rather than its transgressive quality.

16. Critics have commented on Marion's smile when she imagines Cassidy saying he will take the money out of her flesh. Her smile is later echoed by Norman's final smile as Mother. As Barbara Klinger argues, the film makes us initially think that Marion is the psycho of the film's title, in her argument relating female sexuality to the abnormal (51). Wood sees the verdict on herself as "hideously disproportionate to the crime" (145). Rothman suggests that Marion's smirk may conceal a desire to avenge herself on Cassidy, and possibly on Sam (269).

17. Critics have also noted the doubling between Sam and Norman. Toles notes that the "the rasping sound of the venetian blinds as Sam jerks them up matches the sound and motion of the shower curtain being torn open" (644). Corber argues that Sam and Norman are both linked as the murderers of Marion: "Sam's unwillingness to marry Marion prevents her from achieving the American dream and thus constitutes a kind of murder" (215).

18. Paula Marantz Cohen argues that "Norman's mother is not guilty of anything as far as we can tell, despite what the pontificating psychiatrist at the end would have us believe. It is Norman's imagination of his mother, his projection of an idea onto her corpse, that constitutes Mrs. Bates in the film" (148). Bauso sees Mrs. Bates as "the archetypal unacknowledged victim of American cinema, and it is a sad yet predictable irony that she should ever have been construed as a predator" (13). Rothman notes that when we see inside the Bates' house we see that "the woman elsewhere invoked as a monster momentarily appears before us as human, capable of tenderness and love, a woman whose illness is a heartbreaking human tragedy" (321).

19. Bloch argues that he wrote the novel as a response to a society "growing ever more dangerous, and violence no longer confined to 'criminal elements' in 'bad neighborhoods'" ("Building" 59). Wood argues that *Psycho* is a key work of the postwar world, because its horrors are grounded in an age "that has witnessed on the one hand the discoveries of Freudian psychology and on the other the Nazi concentration camps" (150). Corber sees the film as reflecting the postwar rise of the expert as one to tell Americans "how to organize and manage their everyday life" (188).

Chapter 3

1. Richard Matheson's novel *I Am Legend* (1954) forged a new literary vampire classic, but did so within the framework of intense and historically specific American fears. Matheson's protagonist, Robert Neville, spends his nights battling the vampires that have taken over his world after nuclear war. Both Neville and the vampires that stalk him are repulsive. In the novel the vampire myth does not possess erotic lure, but is used to encode fears concerning radiation contamination and disease. Mark Janovich reads *I Am Legend* as a vampire novel that expresses 1950s fear of conformism. Even in the midst of war and disease and, apparently, the threat of the supernatural, "Neville is a man of preconditioned habit who unquestionably accepts received, common sense notions of normality, and cannot accept or even imagine alternatives. He is a man who is threatened by anything which challenges his assumptions, and regulates his life according to futile and obsessive rituals" (149).

2. John Flynn notes that Fisher's approach to the Dracula myth in *The Horror of Dracula* represented a return to "the roots and rituals of the traditional fairy tale in which good triumphed over evil. He had given the vampire story credibility again" (86).

3. Gregory Waller notes that in the film vampirism "is presented almost as an alternative or even a superior mode of existence" (114). I read this glamorization of the vampire as a sign that he has been divorced from his association with taboo ideologies.

4. Christopher Craft's landmark article on *Dracula* makes much of the vampire mouth, arguing that the mouth subverts traditional gender distinctions: "Furthermore, this mouth, bespeaking the subversion of the stable and lucid distinctions of gender, is the mouth of all vampires, male and female" (109).

5. Gregory A. Waller notes that in *The Horror of Dracula* "the vampire's embrace transforms his victim into an invalid by day and an expectant lover by night, until she dies and rises completely shorn of her social and moral inhibitions" (117).

6. Harry Horner's sf film *Red Planet Mars* (1952) represents a good example of the atheism/belief split that characterized Cold War rhetoric. In this film the godless Soviets experience a religious revival after God's voice is heard on the radio. Although it appears God's voice has been a communist plot, God truly intervenes, convincing the world of the truth of Christian belief.

7. Michael J. Murphy comments that Francis Lerder's performance as Dracula "gives more the flavor of a European spy than of the supernatural vampire" (68). While Murphy does not develop the point, the European spy in 1958 would be, of course, the communist infiltrator, as a big-budget film from the same time period, *North by Northwest* (1959), demonstrates.

Chapter 4

1. In his discussion of the status of the horror film during World War II, Rick Worland notes that horror films were problematic for anti-Nazi propaganda because of their portrayal of non-Western people as "backward and superstitious," associations that "carried the unambiguous stigma of white supremacy" (53).

2. Anti-communist propaganda films routinely portrayed the Soviets as backward. *Red Planet Mars* (1952) illustrates Soviet life by showing the people as superstitious peasants who lived crowded together in a hut. *Invasion, USA* (1952) shows the Soviet invaders drinking whiskey out of the bottle and attempting to rape women.

3. Jean Piel notes that during the 1950s Bataille "saw clearly that the USSR was there as if to awaken the world, and that America, actually feeling the effect of this permanent threat, began to awaken to an awareness" (105).

4. Fear of reverse imperialism is common in Victorian Gothic works such as *Dracula*, "The Adventure of the Speckled Band," *The Beetle*, *The Lair of the White Worm*, and others. See Stephen D. Arata for an interesting discussion of reverse imperialism in *Dracula*.

Chapter 5

1. Jack Arnold's *The Incredible Shrinking Man* (1957) looks at atomic mutation at the level of the home. *Man* tells the story of Scott Carey, an advertising executive, who, due to a combination of insecticide and radiation, begins

shrinking. The shrinking process is temporarily arrested by doctors, but begins again, and Scott becomes so small that he must live in a dollhouse. After nearly being killed by his pet cat, Scott falls into the basement of his house, where he is forced to live in a matchbox and battle a spider for food. Scott eventually kills the spider, but continues to shrink, moving on to a microcosmic existence at the end of the film.

2. Mark Jancovich argues that Manning has chosen his isolation by trying to save the pilot and, earlier, by enlisting in the Korean War: "He is therefore an individualistic loner who refuses to accept discipline from above, and rejects the comforts of the domestic sphere for the more masculine activities of war" (202). It seems to me, however, that he does not so much reject the domestic and discipline, but, rather, tries to live up to what an ideal man should be: brave and self-sacrificing in any situation. The film charts the failure of that ideal.

3. The deliberate exposure of hundreds of thousands of U.S. soldiers to radiation in order to test the survivability of nuclear war is now well documented. Between the years of 1950 and 1962, the Nevada Test Site was the center of these experiments. During the Desert Rock I Test, the AEC (Atomic Energy Commission) endorsed the Department of Defense's suggestion that troops be stationed four miles from ground zero, despite the fact that the AEC imposed a seven-mile limit on its own personnel (*Human* 298). The exposure of servicemen to unacceptable doses of radiation in these tests was predicated on a notion that nuclear war would be fought on the conventional battlefield as well. See also Eileen Welsome's book *The Plutonium Files: America's Secret Medical Experiments in the Cold War.*

4. Jancovich notes that even though Glenn is transformed into a true monster in the sequel, "the film manages to evoke some sympathy for him at the end" (204).

5. Mothers were also frequently held responsible for negative nonconformist behavior in men. As George Chauncey, Jr. notes in his discussion of the postwar sex crime panic, "Mothers took much of the blame . . . Such warnings implied that the women who failed to follow psychiatrists' advice had only themselves to blame for the men who attacked them and their children" (172).

6. Whyte perceived Freudian psychology as abetting corporate conformity through the form of the personality test. He cites the case of a twenty-eight-year-old man married to a thirty-year-old woman about whom corporate psychologists concluded that "may have been influenced in marrying her by unconsciously considering her as a mother-surrogate . . . may be inclined to be passive-dependent—i.e., reliant on others for direction and guidance—in his general work relationships" (192).

7. Michael Rogin examines the influence of momism on cold war popular culture. His article argues that frequently lurking beneath cold war films' suspicion of communism is a suspicion of the mother.

8. *Invasion of the Body Snatchers* (1956) is the classic example of the fear of a mass mind destroying individualism. Other sf/horror films in this vein include *It Came from Outer Space, Invaders from Mars, I Married a Monster from Outer Space*, and *Killers from Space*.

Chapter 7

1. Typically, our dominant perception of the fifties juvenile delinquent is directed upon the male criminal: representations in fifties films tend to focus on the problem of the bad boy. However, there was a culture of female juvenile delinquency that garnered some attention in fifties America. Rachel Devlin argues that female juvenile delinquency was portrayed as "only incipient in nature and largely hidden from view" (85). Wini Breines also explores the issue of female delinquency, discussing white girls' use of "the sensibilities of darkness as a way out of boredom and restlessness" ("Postwar White Girls" 71). This issue is explored at more length in her book-length study *Young, White and Miserable: Growing up Female in the Fifties*. For a discussion of the subgenre of the teen horror film, see Thomas Doherty's *Teenagers and Teenpics*.

2. Many commentators on fifties culture notice the excoriation of the father in sociological studies and in popular culture. Devlin comments on the fifties "sense of disappointment in the American father" (97). Gaile McGregor's view is that so far as the fifties were concerned, "familial breakdown is in the end the father's responsibility—in short, his *fault*" (12). In his discussion of *Rebel without a Cause*, Thomas Leitch cites the "poor example of his father" as Jim's primary problem (44). Conversely, and specific to the film, Nina C. Leibman views *Rebel without a Cause* as an illustration of Philip Wylie's concept of Momism, arguing that the agenda of the film is "to render Wylie's dastardly mothers in all their configurations" (211). I disagree, viewing the film as one that traces problems of the mother ultimately to the failure of paternal authority. If mom is bad or absent, it's dad's fault, the film tells us.

3. One frequent point made by commentators on fifties juvenile delinquency is its apolitical motivations. Lindner's title, *Rebel without a Cause*, stems from his belief that the teen criminal is "an agitator without a slogan, a revolutionary without a program" (2). David Halberstam, commenting on fifties rebels, states that "there was little overt political content in their rebellion" (479). While Almond does link delinquency to communism, he argues that American teenagers who joined the party did so out of apolitical motivations: they believed they were "affiliating themselves with something that is esoteric, outlawed, iconoclastic, pitted against society" (231).

4. Joseph Reed argues that Tony represents "every teenager." He sees Tony's transformation as one that any teenager could identify with: "The Change, those moments when Werewolf passes from human to beast, parallels puberty's confusion and horror" (133-34). I disagree. Tony's behavior is aber-

rant in the film both before and after the transformation. The film takes pains to distinguish him from the other teens, as his behavior, especially at the party where he beats up his best friend, Vic, indicates.

5. Of *Rebel without a Cause*, Leitch argues that "although individual parents may fail in *Rebel without a Cause*, adult values are affirmed throughout the film" (44).

6. Mark Jancovich argues that the adult world's perception of Tony is summed up in the principal's statement that the school needs to "really get inside" Tony. As Jancovich argues, "The notion of 'really getting inside' Tony implies intrusion, control, and even brainwashing, an implication which is confirmed by the activities of the psychiatrist, Dr. Brandon" (208-09). I agree: Brandon is really just a sinister, but logical, extension of the other authority figures who appear in the film.

Chapter 8

1. See Barbara Creed's extensive study of the monstrous-feminine in horror films in her book *The Monstrous-Feminine: Film, Feminism, Psychoanalysis*.

2. While the femme fatale of such Forties noir classics was not as prevalent in fifties films, partly due to science-fiction and horror films' overtaking the popularity of crime films in the decade, she still lurked, and linked female sexuality with a subversive political threat. Michael Rogin, for examples, argues that the figure of the dangerous female appeared in such cold war films as *Kiss Me, Deadly* and *The Manchurian Candidate* because the political consciousness of these films was "subordinate to its sexual unconsciousness" (29).

3. Strecker and Lathbury cite numerous examples of girls whose lives have been damaged by maternal misguidance in *Their Mothers' Daughters*. One woman interviewed found herself unable to enjoy sex with her husband. The authors relate that after "a long and painful course of treatment" analysts discovered that when the woman was a child her mother had remarked about the "nastiness of sex" and "the vileness and selfishness of men" (136). These comments supposedly scarred the girl and made her frigid in her life as a married woman.

4. In his autobiography, Corman relates that he used the same filmed sequence of the burning of the house of Usher in his 1960 film *House of Usher* for other films as well. The climax of "Morella" is a repetition of the ending of Usher, even down to the use of the same footage. In *Usher*, Madeleine is justified in killing Roderick; by contrast, however, Morella's act seems vindictive and unnecessary.

Works Cited

The Alligator People. Dir. Roy Del Ruth. 20th-Century Fox, 1959.

Almond, Gabriel A. *The Appeals of Communism.* Princeton: Princeton UP, 1954.

The Amazing Colossal Man. Dir. Bert I. Gordon. American International, 1957.

Arata, Stephen D. "The Occidental Tourist: *Dracula* and the Anxiety of Reverse Colonization." *Victorian Studies* (Summer 1990): 627-34.

The Astounding She-Monster. Dir. Ronnie Ashcroft. AIP, 1958.

Auerbach, Nina. *Our Vampires, Ourselves.* Chicago: U of Chicago P, 1995.

Aulier, Dan. *Vertigo: The Making of a Hitchcock Classic.* New York: St. Martin's, 1998.

The Bad Seed. Dir. Mervyn LeRoy. Warner, 1956.

Bataille, Georges. *The Accursed Share.* Vols. II and III. Trans. Robert Hurley. New York: Zone, 1993.

——. *Erotism: Death and Sensuality.* Trans. Mary Dalwood. San Francisco: City Lights, 1986.

——. *Guilty.* Trans. Bruce Boone. Venice, CA: Lapis, 1988.

——. *The Impossible.* Trans. Robert Hurley. San Francisco: City Lights, 1991.

——. *Literature and Evil.* Trans. Alastair Hamilton. New York: Marion Boyars, 1997.

——. *The Tears of Eros.* 1961. Trans. Peter Connor. San Francisco: City Lights, 1989.

——. *Theory of Religion.* Trans. Robert Hurley. New York: Zone, 1989.

——. *Visions of Excess: Selected Writings, 1927-1939.* Trans. and ed. Allan Stoekl. Minneapolis: U of Minnesota P, 1985.

Bauso, Tom. "Mother Knows Best: The Voices of Mrs. Bates in *Psycho.*" *Hitchcock Annual* 1994: 3-17.

Baym, Nina. "Melodramas of Beset Manhood: How Theories of American Fiction Exclude Women Authors." *Feminist Criticism: Essays on Women, Literature, and Theory.* Ed. Elaine Showalter. New York: Pantheon, 1985. 63-80.

Bellour, Raymond. "Psychosis, Neurosis, Perversion." Trans. Nancy Huston. *Camera Obscura* 2 (Fall 1979): 105-34.

Benshoff, Harry M. *Monsters in the Closet: Homosexuality and the Horror Film.* Manchester: Manchester UP, 1997.

Besnier, Jean-Michel. "Bataille, The Emotive Intellectual." *Bataille: Writing the Sacred.* Ed. Carolyn Bailey Gill. New York: Routledge, 1995. 12-25.

The BFI Companion to Horror. Ed. Kim Newman. London: Cassell, 1996.

Biskind, Peter. *Seeing Is Believing: How Hollywood Taught Us to Stop Worrying and Love the Fifties.* New York: Pantheon, 1983.

Bloch, Robert. "Building the Bates Motel." *Mystery Scene* 40.19 (1993): 26-27, 58.

———. *Psycho.* 1959. New York: TOR, 1989.

Bolieau, Pierre, and Thomas Narcejac. *The Living and the Dead.* Trans. Geoffrey Sainsbury. New York: Washburn, 1957.

Botting, Fred, and Scott Wilson. Introduction. *Bataille: A Critical Reader.* Ed. Fred Botting and Scott Wilson. Oxford: Blackwell, 1998. 1-23.

Breines, Wini. "Postwar White Girls' Dark Others." *The Other Fifties: Interrogating Midcentury American Icons.* Ed. Joel Foreman. Urbana: U of Illinois P, 1996. 53-77.

———. *Young, White, and Miserable: Growing up Female in the Fifties.* Boston: Beacon, 1992.

The Brides of Dracula. Dir. Terence Fisher. Hammer, 1960.

Brill, Leslie. *The Hitchcock Romance: Love and Irony in Hitchcock's Films.* Princeton: Princeton UP, 1988.

Bronfen, Elisabeth. *Over Her Dead Body: Death, Femininity, and the Aesthetic.* New York: Routledge, 1992.

———. "Risky Resemblances: On Repetition, Mourning, and Representation." *Death and Representation.* Ed. Sarah Webster Goodwin and Elisabeth Bronfen. Baltimore: Johns Hopkins UP, 1993. 103-29.

Brottman, Mikita. "Ritual, Tension, and Relief: The Terror of *The Tingler*." *Film Quarterly* 50.4 (Summer 1997): 2-10.

Brown, Harrison. *Must Destruction Be Our Destiny?* New York: Simon and Schuster, 1946.

Brown, Royal S. "Vertigo as Orphic Tragedy." *Literature/Film Quarterly* 14 (1986): 32-43.

Bryers, Thomas B. "Kissing Becky: Masculine Fears and Misogynist Moments in Science Fiction Films." *Arizona Quarterly* 45.3 (Autumn 1989): 77-95.

Burgess, Ernest W., and Paul Wallin. *Engagement and Marriage.* Chicago: Lippincott, 1953.

Chankin, Donald O. "Delusions and Dreams in Hitchcock's Vertigo." *Hitchcock Annual* (1993): 28-40.

Chauncey, George, Jr. "The Postwar Sex Crime Panic." *True Stories from the American Past.* Ed. William Graebner. New York: McGraw-Hill, 1993. 160-78.

Children of the Damned. Dir. Anton Leader. MGM, 1963.

Clark, William L. " 'The Kids Really Fit': Rock Text and Rock Practice in Bill Haley's Rock Around the Clock." *Popular Music and Society* 18.4 (1994): 57-76.

Cohen, Paula Marantz. *Alfred Htichcock: The Legacy of Victorianism.* Lexington: UP of Kentucky, 1995.

Corber, Robert J. *In The Name of National Security: Hitchcock, Homophobia, and the Political Construction of Gender in Postwar America.* Durham: Duke UP, 1993.

Corman, Roger. With Jim Jerome. *How I Made a Hundred Movies in Hollywood and Never Lost a Dime.* New York: Random, 1990.

Craft, Christopher. "'Kiss Me with Those Red Lips': Gender and Inversion in Bram Stoker's *Dracula.*" *Representations* 8 (Fall 1984): 107-33.

Creed, Barbara. *The Monstrous-Feminine: Film, Feminism, Psychoanalysis.* New York: Routledge, 1993.

Crowther, Bosley. "An Answer to Those Filmgoers Who Think '*Psycho*' Should Be Banned." *New York Times* 28 Aug. 1960. *New York Times* Online. Available: http://www.nytimes/com/library/film/082860hitch-psycho-ban/html 2 May 1999.

Cult of the Cobra. Dir. Francis D. Lyon. Universal, 1955.

Curse of the Mummy's Tomb. Dir. Michael Carreras. Hammer, 1964.

Curse of the Undead. Dir. Edward Dein. Universal, 1959.

"A Decision for Mankind." *St. Louis Post-Dispatch* 7 Aug. 1945.

The Decline of the American Male. By the editors of *Look* magazine. New York: Random, 1958.

Devlin, Rachel. "Female Juvenile Delinquency and the Problem of Sexual Authority in America, 1945-1965." *Delinquents and Debutantes: Twentieth Century Girls' Cultures.* Ed. Sherrie Inness. New York: New York UP, 1998. 83-105.

Doherty, Thomas. *Teenagers and Teenpics: The Juvenilization of American Movies in the 1950s.* Boston: Unwin Hyman, 1988.

Donohue, H. E. F. "Remembrance of Murders Past: An Interview with Alfred Hitchcock." *New York Times* 14 Dec. 1969. *New York Times* Online. Available: http://www.nytimes/com/library/film/121469hitch-interview.html 2 May 1999.

Douglas, William O. "The Black Silence of Fear." *The Age of McCarthyism: A Brief History with Documents.* By Ellen Schrecker. Boston: Bedford, 1994. 243-46.

Dragon, Jean. "The Work of Alterity: Bataille and Lacan." *Diacritics* 26.2 (Summer 1996): 31-48.

Ehrenreich, Barbara. *The Hearts of Men: American Dreams and the Flight from Commitment.* New York: Doubleday, 1983.

Ellis, Albert. *The American Sexual Tragedy.* New York: Twayne, 1954.

Fine, Benjamin. *1,000,000 Delinquents.* Cleveland: World, 1955.

Finney, Jack. *Invasion of the Body Snatchers.* Rpt. of *The Body Snatchers.* 1955. New York: Simon and Schuster, 1978.

First Man into Space. Dir. Robert Day. Amalgamated Productions, 1959.

Flesh and Blood: The Hammer Heritage of Horror. Dir. Ted Newsom. Heidelberg Films, 1997.

The Fly. Dir. Kurt Neumann. 20th Century Fox, 1958.

Flynn, John L. *Cinematic Vampires: The Living Dead on Film and Television, from 'The Devil's Castle' (1896) to 'Bram Stoker's Dracula' (1992).* Jefferson, NC: McFarland, 1992.

Gasché, Rodolphe. "The Heterological Almanac." *On Bataille: Critical Essays.* Ed. and trans. Leslie Anne Boldt-Irons. Albany: SUNY, 1995. 157-208.

The Giant Gila Monster. Dir. Ray Kellogg. McLendon Radio Pictures, 1959.

Gordon, Joan, and Veronica Hollinger. "Introduction: The Shape of Vampires." *Blood Read: The Vampire as Metaphor in Contemporary Culture.* Ed. Joan Gordon and Veronica Hollinger. Philadelphia: U of Pennsylvania P, 1997. 1-7.

Gorer, Geoffrey. *The American People: A Study in National Character.* New York: Norton, 1948.

Griffith, Robert. "American Politics and the Origins of 'McCarthyism.'" *A History of Our Time: Readings on Postwar America.* 2nd ed. Ed. William H. Chafe and Harvard Sitkoff. New York: Oxford UP, 1987. 51-63.

Halberstam, David. *The Fifties.* New York: Villard, 1993.

Hendershot, Cyndy. "The Invaded Body: Paranoia and Radiation Anxiety in *Invaders from Mars, It Came from Outer Space,* and *Invasion of the Body Snatchers.*" *Extrapolation* 39.1 (1998): 26-39.

———. "Vampire and Replicant: The One-Sex Body in a Two-Sex World." *Science-Fiction Studies* 22.3 (1995): 373-98.

Hoberek, Andrew P. "The 'Work' of Science Fiction: Philip K. Dick and Occupational Masculinity in the Post-World War II United States." *Modern Fiction Studies* 43.2 (1997): 374-404.

Hodgens, Richard. "A Short Tragical History of the Science Fiction Film." 1959. *SF: The Other Side of Realism: Essays on Modern Fantasy and Science Fiction.* Ed. Thomas D. Clareson. Bowling Green, OH: Bowling Green State U Popular P, 1971. 248-62.

Hofstadter, Richard. "The Paranoid Style in American Politics." *The Paranoid Style in American Politics and Other Essays.* New York: Knopf, 1966. 3-40.

Hogan, David J. *Dark Romance: Sexuality in the Horror Film.* Jefferson, NC: McFarlandy, 1986.

Hoggart, Richard. *The Uses of Literacy.* New York: Oxford UP, 1957.

Hollings, Ken. "In the Slaughterhouse of Love." *My Mother/Madame Edwarda/The Dead Man.* By Georges Bataille. Trans. Austryn Wainhouse. New York: Marion Boyars, 1995. 199-214.

Hoover, J. Edgar. "Testimony before HUAC, March 26, 1947." *The Age of McCarthyism: A Brief History with Documents*. By Ellen Schrecker. Boston: Bedford, 1994. 114-20.

The Horror of Dracula. Dir. Terence Fisher. Hammer, 1958.

Horrors of the Black Museum. Dir. Arthur Crabtree. American International, 1959.

House of Usher. Dir. Roger Corman. AIP, 1960.

House of Wax. Dir. André De Toth. Warner Brothers, 1953.

The Human Radiation Experiments: Final Report of the Advisory Committee on Human Radiation Experiments. New York: Oxford UP, 1996.

I Was a Teenage Werewolf. Dir. Gene Fowler, Jr. American International, 1957.

"Interview with Edward Teller." Lawrence Livermore National Laboratory. Online. Available: http://www.llnl.gov 2 June 1996.

Invasion of the Body Snatchers. Dir. Don Siegel. Allied Artists, 1956.

It! The Terror from Beyond Space. Dir. Edward L. Cahn. Vogue, 1958.

Jancovich, Mark. *Rational Fears: American Horror in the 1950s*. Manchester: Manchester UP, 1996.

Johnson, Glen. "'We'd Fight . . . We Had to': *The Body Snatchers* as Novel and Film." *Journal of Popular Culture* 13.1 (Summer 1979): 5-14.

Kaminsky, Stuart M. "Don Siegel on the Pod Society." *Invasion of the Body Snatchers*. Ed. Al La Valley. New Brunswick: Rutgers UP, 1989. 153-57.

Keane, Marian. "A Closer Look at Scopophilia: Mulvey, Hitchcock, and *Vertigo*." *A Hitchcock Reader*. Ed. Marshall Deutebaum and Leland Poague. Ames: Iowa State UP, 1986. 231-48.

King, Stephen. Foreword. *Night Shift*. New York: Signet, 1979. xi-xxii.

Klinger, Barbara. "*Psycho*: The Institutionalization of Female Sexuality." *Wide Angle* 5.1 (1982): 49-55.

Knee, Adam. "The Metamorphosis of the Fly." *Wide Angle* 14.1 (Jan. 1992): 20-34.

Krupnick, Mark. "Lionel Trilling, Freud, and the Fifties." *Humanities in Society* 3.3 (1980): 265-81.

Langelaan, George. "The Fly." 1957. *Reel Future*. Ed. Forrest J. Ackerman and Jean Stine. New York: Barnes and Noble, 1994. 343-71.

Lawrence, D. H. "Edgar Allan Poe." *Twentieth Century Interpretations of the Fall of the House of Usher*. Ed. Thomas Woodson. Englewood Cliffs, NJ: Prentice-Hall, 1969.

The Leech Woman. Dir. Edward Dein. Universal, 1959.

Le Gacy, Arthur. "*Invasion of the Body Snatchers*: A Metaphor for the Fifties." *Literature/Film Quarterly* 6.3 (1978): 285-92.

Leibman, Nina. C. *Living Room Lectures: The Fifties Family in Film and Television*. Austin: U of Texas P, 1995.

Leigh, Janet. With Christopher Nickens. *Psycho: Behind the Scenes of the Classic Thriller.* New York: Harmony, 1995.

Leitch, Thomas. "The World According to Teenpix." *Literature/Film Quarterly* 20.1 (1992): 43-47.

"Letters to the Screen Editor: 'Psycho' Analysis by Mail." *New York Times* 31 July 1960. *New York Times* Online. Available: http://www.nytimes.com/library/film/073160hitch-psycho-letters.html 2 May 1999.

Levenstein, Aaron. *The Atomic Age: Suicide . . . Slavery or Social Planning?* New York: League for Industrial Democracy, 1946.

Linderman, Deborah. "The Mise-En-Abime in Hitchcock's *Vertigo.*" *Cinema Journal* 30.4 (Summer 1991): 51-74.

Lindner, Robert. *Rebel without a Cause.* New York: Grove, 1944.

MacKenzie, Gordene Olga. *Transgender Nation.* Bowling Green, OH: Bowling Green State U Popular P, 1994.

Mainwaring, Daniel. *Invasion of the Body Snatchers.* Ed. Al La Valley. New Brunswick: Rutgers UP, 1989. 31-109.

Man Beast. Dir. Jerry Warren. Jerry Warren, 1956,

March, William. *The Bad Seed.* Hopewell, NJ: Ecco, 1997.

Matheson, Richard. *I Am Legend.* 1954. New York: TOR, 1995.

Matta, George. "Bean Camp." The Korean War Project. Online. Available: http://www.koreanwar.org/html/units/frontline/chap2.htm Sept. 9 1998.

McClay, Wilfred. "Fifty Years of the Lonely Crowd." *Wilson Quarterly* 22.3 (1998): 34-42.

McGregor, Gaile. "Domestic Blitz: A Revisionist History of the Fifties." *American Studies* 34.1 (Spring 1993): 5-33.

Merrick. James W. "Hitchcock Regime for a 'Psycho.'" *New York Times* 27 Dec. 1959. *New York Times* Online. Available: http://www.nytimes.com/library/film/073160hitch-psycho-making.html 2 May 1999.

Meyerowitz, Joanne. "Beyond the Feminine Mystique: A Reassessment of Postwar Mass Culture, 1946-1958." *Journal of American History* 79.4 (Mar. 1993): 1455-82.

Miller, Arthur. *The Crucible.* 1953. New York: Penguin, 1984.

Modelski, Tania. *The Women Who Knew Too Much: Hitchcock and Feminist Theory.* New York: Methuen, 1988.

Monster on the Campus. Dir. Jack Arnold. Universal, 1958.

Morris, Gary. *Roger Corman.* Boston: Twayne, 1985.

Mumford, Lewis. "Gentlemen, You Are Mad!" *Saturday Review of Literature* 2 Mar. 1946: 5-6.

——. *In the Name of Sanity.* New York: Harcourt, Brace, 1954.

The Mummy. Dir. Terence Fisher. Hammer, 1959.

Murphy, Michael J. *The Celluloid Vampires: A History and Filmography: 1897-1979.* Ann Arbor: Pierian, 1979.

Nader, Laura. "The Phantom Factor: Impact of the Cold War on Anthropology." *The Cold War and the University: Toward an Intellectual History of the Postwar Years*. Ed. Noam Chomsky, et al. New York: New, 1997. 107-46.

Newman, Kim. Introduction. *The BFI Companion to Horror*. Ed. Kim Newman. London: Cassell, 1996. 11-16.

Oakley, Ronald J. *God's Country: America in the Fifties*. New York: Dembner, 1986.

Paul, William. *Laughing Screaming: Modern Hollywood Horror and Comedy*. New York: Columbia UP, 1994.

Perry, Dennis R. "Imps of the Perverse: Discovering the Poe/Hitchcock Connection." *Literature/Film Quarterly* 24.4 (1996): 393-99.

Phantom of the Rue Morgue. Dir. Roy Del Ruth. Warner, 1954.

Phillips, Louis. "*Vertigo*: After Such Knowledge, What Forgiveness?" *Armchair Detective* 17.4 (Spring 1984): 188-91.

Piel, Jean. "Bataille and the World from 'The Notion of Expenditure' to *The Accursed Share*." *On Bataille: Critical Essays*. Ed. and trans. Leslie Anne Boldt-Irons. Albany: SUNY, 1995. 96-106.

Pietz, William. "The 'Post-Colonialism' of Cold War Discourse." *Social Text* 19-20 (Fall 1988): 55-75.

Poznar, Walter. "Orpheus Descending: Love in *Vertigo*." *Literature/Film Quarterly* 17 (1989): 59-65.

Prawler, S. S. *Caligari's Children: The Film as Tale of Terror*. New York: Oxford UP, 1980.

Psycho. Dir. Alfred Hitchcock. Universal, 1960.

Rawlings, Jack P. "Confronting the Alien: Fantasy and Anti-Fantasy in Science Fiction Film and Literature." *Bridges to Fantasy*. Ed. George Edgar Slusser, Eric S. Rabkin, and Robert E. Scholes. Carbondale: Southern Illinois UP, 1982. 160-74.

Reed, Joseph W. *American Scenarios: The Uses of Film Genre*. Middletown, CT: Weslyan UP, 1989.

The Return of Dracula. Dir. Paul Landres. United Artists, 1958.

Richardson, Michael. *Georges Bataille*. New York: Routledge, 1994.

Rieff, Philip. *Freud: The Mind of the Moralist*. 1959. New York: Anchor, 1961.

Riesman, David. "Innocence of the Lonely Crowd." *Society* (1998): 339-42.

——. *The Lonely Crowd: A Study of the Changing American Character*. New Haven: Yale UP, 1950.

Rogin, Michael. "*Kiss Me Deadly*: Communism, Motherhood, and Cold War Movies." *Representations* 6 (Spring 1984): 1-36.

Rothman, William. *Hitchcock—The Murderous Gaze*. Cambridge: Harvard UP, 1982.

Said, Edward. *Orientalism*. New York: Pantheon, 1978.

Samuels, Stuart. "The Age of Conspiracy and Conformity: *Invasion of the Body Snatchers." American History/American Film: Interpreting the Hollywood Image.* Ed. John E. O'Connor and Martin A. Jackson. New York: Ungar, 1979. 203-17.

Sasso, Robert. "Georges Bataille and the Challenge to Think." *On Bataille: Critical Essays.* Ed. and trans. Leslie Anne Boldt-Irons. Albany: SUNY, 1995. 41-49.

Schrecker, Ellen. *The Age of McCarthyism: A Brief History with Documents.* Boston: Bedford, 1994.

Seed, David. "Alien Invasions by Body Snatchers and Related Creatures." *Modern Gothic: A Reader.* Ed. Victor Sage and Allan Lloyd Smith. Manchester: Manchester UP, 1996. 152-70.

Sharrett, Christopher. "The Myth of Apocalypse and the Horror Film: The Primacy of *Psycho* and *The Birds." Hitchcock Annual* 1995-1996: 38-60.

Showalter, Elaine. Introduction. *The Bad Seed.* By William March. Hopewell, NJ: Ecco, 1997.

Simmonds, Roy S. *The Two Worlds of William March.* Tuscaloosa, AL: U of Alabama P, 1984.

Simmons, Jerold. "The Production Code Under New Management: Geoffrey Shurlock, *The Bad Seed,* and *Tea and Sympathy." Journal of Popular Film and Television* 22.1 (Spring 1994): 2-10.

Simper, DeLoy. "Poe, Hitchcock, and the Well-Wrought Effect." *Literature/ Film Quarterly* 3 (1975): 225-31.

Snatchers." *American History/American Film: Interpreting the Hollywood Image.* Ed. John E. O'Connor and Martin A. Jackson. New York: Frederick Ungar, 1979. 203-17.

Steffen-Fluhr, Nancy. "Women and the Inner Game of Don Siegel's *Invasion of the Body Snatchers." Invasion of the Body Snatchers.* Ed. Al La Valley. New Brunswick: Rutgers UP, 1989. 206-21.

Stoker, Bram. *Dracula.* Ed. Nina Auerbach and David J. Skal. New York: Norton, 1997.

Stone, I. F. *The Haunted Fifties.* Boston: Little, Brown, 1963.

Strecker, Edward A., and Vincent T. Lathbury. *Their Mothers' Daughters.* Philadelphia: Lippincott, 1956.

Surkis, Judith. "No Fun and Games Until Someone Loses an Eye: Transgression and Masculinity in Bataille and Foucault." *Diacritics* 26.2 (Summer 1996): 18-30.

Tales of Terror. Dir. Roger Corman. AIP, 1962.

Terry, Jennifer. "'Momism' and the Making of Treasonous Homosexuals." *"Bad" Mothers: The Politics of Blame in Twentieth-Century America.* Ed. Molly Ladd-Taylor and Lauri Umansky. New York: New York UP, 1998. 169-90.

The Tingler. Dir. William Castle. Columbia, 1959.

Toles, George. "'If Thine Eye Offend Thee . . .': Psycho and the Art of Infection." *New Literary History* 15.3 (Spring 1984): 631-51.

Truffaut, Francois. *Hitchcock.* Rev. ed. New York: Simon and Schuster, 1983.

Trumpener, Katie. "Fragments of the Mirror: Self-Reference, Mise-en-Abyme, *Vertigo.*" *Hitchcock's ReReleased Films: From Rope to Vertigo.* Ed. Walter Raubicheck and Walter Srebnick. Detroit: Wayne State UP, 1991. 175-88.

Tudor, Andrew. "Why Horror? The Peculiar Pleasures of a Popular Genre." *Cultural* Studies 11.3 (1997): 443-63.

Vertigo. Dir. Alfred Hitchcock. Paramount, 1958.

Village of the Damned. Dir. Wolf Rilla. MGM, 1960.

Waller, Gregory A. *The Living and the Undead: From Stoker's 'Dracula' to Romero's 'Dawn of the Dead.'* Urbana: U of Illinois P, 1986.

Wallerstein, Immanuel. "The Unintended Consequences of Cold War Area Studies." *The Cold War and the University: Toward an Intellectual History of the Postwar Years.* Ed. Noam Chomsky, et al. New York: New, 1997. 195-231.

The War of the Colossal Beast. Dir. Bert I. Gordon. American International, 1958.

Weart, Spencer. *Nuclear Fear: A History of Images.* Cambridge: Harvard UP, 1988.

Webster, David S. "David Riesman: American Scholar." *Society* 36.4 (1999): 62-66.

Welsome, Eileen. *The Plutonium Files: America's Secret Medical Experiments in the Cold War.* New York: Dial, 1999.

West, Ann. "The Concept of the Fantastic in *Vertigo.*" *Hitchcock's ReReleased Films: From Rope to Vertigo.* Ed. Walter Raubicheck and Walter Srebnick. Detroit: Wayne State UP, 1991. 163-74.

Whyte, William, Jr. *The Organization Man.* New York: Simon and Schuster, 1956.

Williams, Tony. *Hearths of Darkness: The Family in the American Horror Film.* Madison: Farleigh Dickinson UP, 1996.

Wolfson, Adam. "Individualism: New and Old." *The Public Interest* 15 Jan. 1997.

Wollen, Peter. "Compulsion." *Sight and Sound* Apr. 1997: 14-18.

Wood, Robin. *Hitchcock's Films Revisited.* New York: Columbia UP, 1989.

——. "Male Desire, Male Anxiety: The Essential Hitchcock." *A Hitchcock Reader.* Ed. Marshall Deutebaum and Leland Poague. Ames: Iowa State UP, 1986. 219-30.

Worland, Rick. "OWI Meets Monsters: Hollywood Horror Films and War Propaganda, 1942 to 1945." *Cinema Journal* 37.1 (Fall 1997): 47-65.

Wylie, Philip. *Generation of Vipers.* 1942. New York: Rinehart, 1955.

X: The Unknown. Dir. Leslie Norman. Hammer, 1956.

Yvard, P. "Literature and Society in the Fifties in Great Britain." *Journal of European Studies* 3 (1973): 36-44.

INDEX

CPSIA information can be obtained
at www.ICGtesting.com
Printed in the USA
FFOW04n1954061216
30017FF